reading the RIOT ACT

Other books by the author

POETRY
Accidence (OUTSIDE PRESS)
On the Ropes (COACH HOUSE BOOKS)
Works that way because that's the way it works
(TSUNAMI EDITIONS)

TRANSLATION
Gabriel Dumont Speaks (TALONBOOKS)

ANTHOLOGY
*Writing Class: The Kootenay School of Writing
Anthology* (NEW STAR BOOKS)

reading the RIOT ACT

A BRIEF HISTORY OF RIOTS IN VANCOUVER

MICHAEL BARNHOLDEN

Anvil Press | Vancouver | 2005

Copyright © 2005 Michael Barnholden

All rights reserved. No part of this book may be reproduced by any means without the prior written permission of the publisher, with the exception of brief passages in reviews. Any request for photocopying or other reprographic copying of any part of this book must be directed in writing to Access Copyright: The Canadian Copyright Licensing Agency, One Yonge Street, Suite 1900, Toronto, Ontario, Canada, M5E 1E5.

LIBRARY AND ARCHIVES CANADA CATALOGUING IN PUBLICATION

Barnholden, Michael, 1951-
    Reading the riot act : a brief history of riots in Vancouver / Michael Barnholden.

Includes bibliographical references and index.
ISBN 1-895636-67-1

    1. Riots–British Columbia–Vancouver. I. Title.
HV6485.C32V35 2005   971.1'33   C2005-901903-4

Printed and bound in Canada
Cover and interior design: Typesmith Design
Represented in Canada by the Literary Press Group
Distributed by University of Toronto Press

The publisher gratefully acknowledges the financial assistance of the B.C. Arts Council, the Canada Council for the Arts, and the Book Publishing Industry Development Program (BPIDP) for their support of our publishing program.

Anvil Press Inc.
PO Box 3008, Main Post Office
Vancouver, B.C.
V6B 3X5
CANADA

Thanks to Nancy Newman, all ways, Neale Barnholden, Patrick Barnholden, Gary Kinsman, Rolf Maurer, Andrew Klobucar, Ted Byrne, Lisa Robertson, Karl Siegler, Colin Smith, Gary Fisher, Roy Miki and the many others who have participated in the discussions leading to this book.

CONTENTS

The Riot Act – British Parliament		9
Preface		13
Introduction		17
Chapter 1	ANTI-ASIAN RIOTS 1907 JAP RIOT 1942	27
Chapter 2	FREE SPEECH RIOTS 1909 & 1911	47
Chapter 3	BLOODY SUNDAY: UNEMPLOYMENT RIOTS OF 1935 & 1938	59
Chapter 4	B.C. PEN RIOTS 1934-1976	75
Chapter 5	GASTOWN RIOT 1971 ROLLING STONES RIOT 1972	87
Chapter 6	SPORTS RIOTS GREY CUP RIOTS 1963 & 1966 STANLEY CUP RIOT 1994	97
Chapter 7	APEC RIOTS 1997 RIOT AT THE HYATT 1998	111
Chapter 8	BRITANNIA RIOT 2002 GUNS N' ROSES RIOT 2002 PUNK ROCK RIOT 2004	123
Conclusion		133
Bibliography		136
Index		139

Policemen assess the damage outside stores on Hastings Street, in the wake of Unemployment riots during the Depression.
LIBRARY AND ARCHIVES CANADA / C-013231

THE RIOT ACT
BRITISH PARLIAMENT

An act for preventing tumults and riotous assemblies, and for the more speedy and effectual punishing of the rioters.

I.

Whereas of late many rebellious riots and tumults have been in divers parts of this kingdom, to the disturbance of the publick peace, and the endangering of his Majesty's person and government, and the same are yet continued and fomented by persons disaffected to his Majesty, presuming so to do, for that the punishments provided by the laws now in being are not adequate to such heinous offences; and by such rioters his Majesty and his administration have been most maliciously and falsly traduced, with an intent to raise divisions, and to alienate the affections of the people from his Majesty therefore for the preventing and suppressing of such riots and tumults, and for the more speedy and effectual punishing the offenders therein; be it enacted by the King's most excellent majesty, by and with the advice and consent of the lords spiritual and temporal and of the commons, in this present parliament assembled, and by the authority of the same, That if any persons to the number of twelve or more, being unlawfully, riotously, and tumultuously assembled together, to the disturbance of the publick peace, at any time after the last day of July in the year of our Lord one thousand seven hundred and fifteen, and being required or commanded by any one or more justice or justices of the peace, or by the sheriff of the county, or his under-sheriff, or by the mayor, bailiff or bailiffs, or other head-officer, or justice of the peace of any city or town corporate, where such assembly shall be, by proclamation to be made in the King's name, in the form herein after directed, to disperse themselves, and peaceably to depart to their habitations, or to their lawful business, shall, to the number of twelve or more (notwithstanding such proclamation made) unlawfully, riotously, and tumultuously remain or continue together by the space of one hour after such command or request made by proclamation, that then such continuing together to the number of twelve or more, after such command or request made by proclamation, shall be adjudged felony without benefit of clergy, and the offenders therein shall be adjudged felons, and shall suffer death as in a case of felony without benefit of clergy.

II.

And be it further enacted by the authority aforesaid, That the order and form of the proclamation that shall be made by the authority of this act, shall be as hereafter followeth (that is to say) the justice of the peace, or other person authorized by this act to make the said proclamation shall, among the said rioters, or as near to them as he can safely come, with a loud voice command, or cause to be commanded silence to be, while proclamation is making, and after that, shall openly and with loud voice make or cause to be made proclamation in these words, or like in effect:

Our sovereign Lord the King chargeth and commandeth all persons, being assembled, immediately to disperse themselves, and peaceably to depart to their habitations, or to their lawful business, upon the pains contained in the act made in the first year of King George, for preventing tumults and riotous assemblies. God save the King.

And every such justice and justices of the peace, sheriff, under-sheriff, mayor, bailiff, and other head-officer aforesaid, within the limits of their respective jurisdictions, are hereby authorized, impowered and required, on notice or knowledge of any such unlawful, riotous and tumultuous assembly, to resort to the place where such unlawful, riotous, and tumultuous assemblies shall be, of persons to the number of twelve or more, and there to make or cause to be made proclamation in manner aforesaid.

[FIRST TWO OF TEN SECTIONS OF THE ORIGINAL RIOT ACT, PASSED 1714, TOOK EFFECT IN AUGUST OF 1715.]

Strikers from unemployment relief camps en route to Eastern Canada during the "March on Ottawa".
LIBRARY AND ARCHIVES CANADA / C-029399

PREFACE

THE WORD *RIOT* comes from obscure origins in Middle English, and originally meant "debate, dispute or argument," but by late Middle English it had come to mean a "violent disturbance of the peace." Later, "riotous" came to mean wanton, loose or debauched, and still does in certain applications, but the meaning of the word has been significantly altered by its presence in the phrase "reading the Riot Act." "Reading the riot act" is a legal phrase that has entered popular culture in a multitude of ways. Parents read their children the riot act, teachers read students the riot act, coaches read players the riot act, and bosses read workers the riot act, all when one—the authority figure—perceives that the other has gotten "out of hand." Bad behaviour, whether it meets the legal definition of the Riot Act or is more akin to the earlier meanings of the word, is seen as riotous and in need of an authority figure to bring proceedings back under control by invoking a higher authority: the Riot Act. Supposedly, the mere mention of the Riot Act is enough to bring hardened miscreants bent on destruction to their collective senses. The act itself is now a seldom-used piece of legislation designed to prevent a riot from taking place. Perhaps in our modern accelerated times, rioters are less hesitant. If the riot has started, it may well be too late to read the Riot Act.

Many different types of riots have entered the popular imagination, ranging from race riots to food riots, from student riots to sport riots; even labour negotiation by riot and its more postmodern expression in the phrase "police riot." Every city has its distinct history of rioting: The Rocket Richard Riots in Montreal, the Christie Pits Riot in Toronto, The Draft Riots in New York City in 1863 and my personal favourite, the Shakespeare Riots in New York in 1849, where rival factions rioted over which actor was the better interpreter of Shakespeare's work. Of course, there is almost always more to the story than meets the eye, but nearly everyone has at least an idea about a local riot that has left its mark on their awareness.

Riots don't happen all that often, which—given my interpretation of the riot as a battle in the class war—continues to amaze me; but when they do, the mainstream discourse is affected for some time following the event. Not that class itself suddenly becomes a topic worthy of consideration, but issues related to class, such as property rights and human rights, come to the fore, often in a reactionary way. Seldom does a point of view like The Clash's proposition that it is, at times, necessary to destroy property, as in the song "Appetite for Destruction," ever get any sympathy in the mainstream, although occasionally important questions do get asked. Usually police brutality becomes the focus, though seldom is the underlying cause examined or given any credence, except when the riot becomes a catalyst for further significant action. Riots are covered in history class at school when they are seen as part of a larger story, such as the Haymarket Riot in Chicago, or the Winnipeg and Regina Riots. The Gastown Riot, followed shortly by the Rolling Stones Riot—which I witnessed—were beginnings for me. I became more interested in the history of rioting in Vancouver during the Stanley Cup Riots of 1994. I had observed some of the action from a distance and was moved to monitor the local, national, and international media coverage, followed by the official reports of the riot, reports that did not match what I had observed or was hearing from both observers and participants. What I noticed is that riots are often part of a larger story when properly contextualized and given careful scrutiny from more than one point of view. I decided to pursue the subject after the APEC riots made it clear that the local political economy was ignored in favour of a "bad apple" explanation, which only further obscured the causes and events leading up to the riot. I have tried to construct a popular history that emphasizes the collective over the individual, group action over great men. For the most part I have relied on secondary sources, but not just official or mainstream reports. I have sought out the record left by participants and observers beyond the usual suspects rounded up by the popular press, and endeavoured to allow the vanquished to have their say. The victors have their history and it serves their purposes. *Reading the Riot Act* is an attempt to reread and rewrite a people's history.

I would fully support and endorse a Vancouver Riot Re-enactment Society, based on the London Riot Re-enactment Society, that would stage re-enactments based on the theme of rioting. Vancouver has a rich history of rioting that could be tapped in order to make these historical events live again. It may not be possible to assemble all the people required to recreate some of the riots of the past, but imagine, if you will, an actor portraying Mayor Gerry McGeer reading the Riot Act to a group of protestors costumed in Depression-era clothes gathered in Victory Square, surrounded by police officers in period riot-squad gear. "Okay boys, you asked for it and here it is." Mayor McGeer reads the Riot Act. After a few seconds of stunned silence the crowd begins singing "The Red Flag" and marches away through the police lines.

> *Then raise the scarlet standard high;*
> *Beneath its folds we'll live and die,*
> *Though cowards flinch and traitors sneer,*
> *We'll keep the red flag flying here.*

Such are the things of dreams.

—MICHAEL BARNHOLDEN
Vancouver, February 2005

16 READING THE RIOT ACT

Street scene during the Winnipeg Strike of 1919.
LIBRARY AND ARCHIVES CANADA / PA-202201

INTRODUCTION

The Sound of Broken Glass
or
If riots are the symptom, Capitalism is the disease

A RIOT, AS DEFINED in s64 of the Criminal Code, is an unlawful assembly that has begun to disturb the peace tumultuously. In s63 (1), an unlawful assembly is an assembly of three or more who, with intent to carry out any common purpose, assemble or conduct themselves when assembled in such a manner to cause persons in the neighbourhood of the assembly on reasonable grounds to believe that they will disturb the peace tumultuously or provoke others to tumultuously disturb the peace. In s63 (2), a lawful assembly can become unlawful when the common purpose becomes unlawful. But when does the peace begin to be disturbed tumultuously? The answer in almost every case is the sound of broken glass, or, at the very least, the fear of glass being broken, which moves the police riot squad to action, and signals the change from an unlawful assembly to the beginning of a riot. Broken glass is a potent image signalling the breakdown of the barrier between public and private property.

The riots that I have looked at for this book have two things in common: police presence beyond the ordinary and an attack on private property, real or imagined. The key question about the riots I have examined always returns to the language of the criminal code: Why would twelve or more persons unlawfully and riotously assemble? Put bluntly, why riot? Surely there are other avenues of negotiation open to the rioters? The Courts could provide remedy to injustices, the legislature can change bad law, the media can expose injustice, and public opinion can compel swift accommodation even in the most recalcitrant. All of these and other various recourses are used by aggrieved parties, but still we have riots. The answer, I have found, lies in looking at the liberal democratic society in which we live and examining how consensus—real or coerced—breaks down. The riot is in itself not the breakdown of social control; it is the penultimate event or crisis in a long drama followed immediately by the reimposition of state control. Democratic order tends to break down over time. Bad public policy—formulated by politicians who cannot or will not listen to the people they are elected to govern—leads to inequities and injustices that popular opinion may oppose. However, often the courts are unable to overrule such shoddy policy, and the process continues, building to an inevitable clash between the state and the disenfranchised. It should be noted that the disenfranchised referred to here are not necessarily marginalized; and, in some instances, part of the rupture can be due to the fact that this particular segment of society is used to having their voice heard.

I have placed great importance on the factors leading up to the riot and the available (i.e. mainstream) analysis in the aftermath, rather than the events of the riots themselves, because I find these circumstances instructive when looked at in a particular way. The first thing that should be noted is this: rarely is anyone killed or permanently injured in a riot; in fact, the very definition of a riot as a disturbance almost precludes acts of violence leading to death. It is most often the rioters themselves who are injured by the police in the act of quelling the riot. Damage to private property is almost always the most significant activity during a riot and should be seen for what it is: an attack on liberal democratic government that places property rights ahead of human rights. Most modern democratic states are based on the philosophy of John Locke, which held that the sole justification for the existence of any government was the preservation of private property. People may starve, their basic human needs may be ignored, so long as the right to private property is maintained.

The riots that we are all familiar with through exposure to the mass media are race riots, food riots, prison riots, labour riots, student riots, youth riots, and ideological riots. What all of these events have in common is that they are essentially episodes in a larger "class war" between the "governed" and their "governors." Not what political economist Eric Hobsbawm called "collective bargaining by riot," but something more. Usually the rioters are demonized and marginalized, or the victims have been demonized or marginalized to the point where somehow their behaviour invites their fate at the hands of the rioters. The classic identifier is the phrase "a few bad apples," which is code for outside agitators (often communists); because good citizens would never disobey a lawful order to disperse, just like the police would never stand back and allow unchallenged attacks on private property. Although the police are there to "serve and protect," they take their orders from duly elected representatives who may have much different values in mind about who exactly they were elected to serve and protect.

> *"All order implies repression"*
> —ROLAND BARTHES

What all these riots have in common is that they are easily identified as episodes of ongoing class conflict between various elements of the working class and the ruling class. Liberal democracies also function as capitalist economies. The most obvious requirement for a governing body to be able to conduct itself in this manner is capital, and the capitalist who owns said capital would prefer that it expand as much as possible and as quickly as possible. There are, of course, limits on that desire, mostly in the form of workers. Capital, in all its permutations and appearances, eventually requires a large number of workers who are ready, willing, and able to perform the bidding of the bosses, preferably at their price. This sets up a contradiction that can never be fully resolved. Who controls the cost of production? Whose needs get met? The need of capital for production (profit) or the need of the worker for reproduction (wages)? And what exactly is the cost of production? It is not difficult to imagine an employer who would prefer slave labour, except for the inordinate responsibility for the slaves' well being that devolves to the owner. What better solution than a system of production where the boss pays as little as possible and takes as little responsibility as possible for the worker? That the minimum wage and forty-hour work week are major concessions wrung from capital with much fighting, and even death, should be remembered whenever the term "class war" is used.

Productivity is the only concern capital has for its workers. Workers must be concerned with their own well being. Property rights versus human rights are the poles of the liberal democratic pendulum. The problem seems obvious: can capitalism be reformed to meet the needs of the majority, or should it function for the benefit of the owners of the means of production? On the one hand the proponents of Corporatism, capitalism's most extreme practice, suggest that reform is not only unnecessary, but harmful. Only the "free" market can provide for all its participants. The other extreme, which takes many forms, calls for the overthrow, or permanent revolution, of both property relations as embodied by private property, and human relations expressed by all forms of privilege. The middle road is, of course, liberalism, whose basic tenet is that capitalism can in fact be reformed. Radicalism is quite obviously excluded by liberalism but the extremes of capitalism are often embraced in an effort to cut the best deal for the largest bloc of voters, thus maintaining power, which is the whole point of the hegemony of capital. Some would argue that controlling workers through trade unions is part of that mechanism, but that is clearly a perversion, not an end in itself. The results of the pendulum swing that liberalism takes us on can be seen in two aspects that are important to this investigation: oppression (defined as keeping workers in a state of misery), and repression (keeping political opposition in a state of powerlessness). In a stable and vibrant economy these aspects become subtle, but never disappear; in a poorly functioning economy, they come to the fore with a vengeance.

CONSENSUS, COERCION AND CONTAINMENT

CONTAINMENT BEGAN AFTER World War II as a policy dedicated to limiting the sphere of influence of communism and led to such tragedies as the War in Vietnam. After the fall of the "Evil Empire," containment was then applied to so-called rogue states such as North Korea, Cuba, Afghanistan, Iran, Iraq, and many other countries who did not completely subscribe to global capitalism. The currently popular phrase used to identify some of these same states is "the axis of evil," with its echoes of

World War II realpolitik. It also has an identifiable domestic parallel that is carried out in much the same way and for much the same reason.

Western democracies depend on the willingness of a large percentage of the population to acquiesce to what is best for capital, which represents the interests of a very small percentage of the population. This consensus is established and maintained in two ways: through intrusion and indifference. Both of these strategies can be administered in many different and subtle ways. The welfare system is an example that combines both intrusion and indifference while institutionalizing poverty and demonizing the poor who use it because they need it. The social welfare system was, in fact, a direct response to the unrest of the 1930s and represents a major compromise on the part of capital with workers. It was a fight to the death for some, just as the struggle for an eight-hour day was for others. Medicare, Worker's Compensation, Unemployment Insurance, and Old Age Pensions all represent compromises that capital has been forced to make in order to ensure their continuation of power and privilege with the collusion of workers. Now in the age of the new world order, the pendulum has swung in the other direction, clawing back these hard-won advances while entrenching new inequities through the use of tactics like part-time employment and contracting out labour.

Coercion takes many forms within this system, the most basic being the paycheque, and the concomitant status that it conveys. A job is the only guarantee within capitalist society of the basic human rights of food and shelter, and there is no right to that. In fact, no mainstream party in our liberal democracy offers even so much as a full employment plank in their electoral platform. This is where property relations meet human relations, and power politics are played out. What is of immediate concern here are the varying groups to whom these "policies"—or, perhaps better viewed as *strategies*—are applied and the net effects of these policies to divide people into "special interest groups" with little or nothing in common. The list of the contained includes labour, students, the young, people of colour, the poor, prisoners, and the ideologically marginal—in other words, those whose class interests are not closely allied to the interests of the controllers of capital. Commentators have become too doctrinaire in their definition of the working class as anyone who has to depend on income not related to an investment of capital. The work is multitudinous and varied, paid and unpaid, but always beholden to the supposed beneficence or charity of capital. This same list defines the participants in the riots I have chosen to study here, because they have one thing in common: their class position. I could find no incidents of the rich rioting for better tax breaks, or against government service cuts. No black-tie riots, no drunken symphony riots, no riots at all.

IF YOU DON'T RIOT YOU CAN'T COMPLAIN

THE MOST TROUBLING riot for me to deal with is the Anti-Asian Riot of 1907, which appears to be the white working class, through their labour and religious organizations, versus the Chinese, Japanese, and Korean workers. But on closer examination of the issues, we can see that white workers were manipulated by the ruling elites, who had no intention of excluding the (oriental) labour they so desperately needed in order to make their business projects profitable. It appears to be one of those situations best illustrated by a quote from John J. Gould: "I can hire one half of the working class to kill the other half."

The free speech fights that consumed the west coast of North America in the 1910s can best be characterized as political riots, in that the ultimate aim of the Industrial Workers of the World was to overthrow capitalism and they demanded the freedom to speak and organize. The response of the ideological state apparatuses, particularly the legislative, judiciary, and police, reveals quite clearly the nature of capitalism's hold. When you add in "free press" and religion to capital's arsenal, the picture becomes even clearer.

What can only be described as food riots in the Dirty Thirties graphically exposed the ultimate nature of capitalism. Men, women, and children starved and lived in the streets and the best the government could do was establish work camps and pathetic relief rations for those willing to comply. These were inadequate band-aids at best. When workers took to the streets to demand "work and wages," they were met with unprecedented levels of violent resistance, both openly in the streets and undercover in the alleys. When governments deploy quasi-military forces against their own citizens, the question must be asked: Whose interest is being served?

The prison riot is perhaps the clearest case of the marginalized taking matters into their own hands. Owning nothing and having no stake in the social contract, but often compelled to work for slave wages or less, the prison system is fertile ground for all types of organizers, with but a few advocating for the abolition of the capitalist system. It is a wonder that people so oppressed can see at all clearly the nature of their oppression.

Youth riots in the late '60s and early '70s are likewise the response of an identifiable cohort denied a place in the world by an economic system dedicated solely to profit, with social programs enacted to keep people in their place. In the case of youth, universal education seems to have had the unfortunate side effect of actually causing some to think and act in regards to their situation. It is interesting to consider the rise of the welfare state with the introduction of welfare, medicare, Unemployment Insurance, and the expansion of educational opportunities after World War II as merely vanguard socialism acting as a brake on the worst excesses of capitalism.

The Stanley Cup Riots are superficially sports riots that, upon closer examination, fit neatly within the realm of class riots as either a consumer or youth riot. It is too easy to dismiss this riot as a party gotten out of hand, with the police called in to protect the innocent owners of private property. Their role as protectors of personal safety for the least able to protect themselves must be questioned. The Stanley Cup Riot marks the passing of Vancouver from a small town to a city-state, declaring itself open for, and to, business. This was a potent political slogan, but also a clear message to workers and other losers in the class warfare that had been waged for the previous ten years. The message was this: "Get out of town or crawl back underground."

Anti-APEC protesters must be seen as dissidents and the riots at UBC and the Hyatt Hotel represent the effort of government to suppress dissent. Although not necessarily anti-capitalist, the anti-globalism rhetoric is fairly clear: human rights and free trade, not free trade followed *maybe* by human rights. The class composition of the protesters is somewhat clouded by the presence of middle-class, relatively privileged protesters. Some of their concern is self-interest, but their protests clearly demonstrate that their interests coincide with those of the working class, because, in fact, they *are* working class; and just as clearly the new world order delineates only between winners and losers, workers and employers/capitalists. What is interesting about their protest is that they are used to having their voices heard and react with something more than mere chagrin when they are denied access to those who are enacting the policies. For the most part, these are not ideologues but pragmatists who want the best for the most. Governing elites are slow to come to terms with the fact that they do not always know what is best for their "subjects." When elected officials get to hang around with dictators as part of their official duties, they tend to get confused and don't quite understand why people get upset with their undemocratic behaviour.

> "The history of British Columbia is a history of class struggle."
>
> —MARK LEIER, *Rebel Life*

ONE OF THE major difficulties I encountered while researching this project was the need to reconcile the press reports and the official accounts of these riots, simply because journalism is, at times, used as an instrument of the ruling class, and as such, is designed to deny any and all class conflict by portraying it as the work of a small minority of malcontents and agitators with no motive short of the thrill of destroying private property. Never is any credence given to the legitimate political aims of such groups as the Industrial Workers of the World in the 1910s, or the Mothers Against Capitalism in the 1930s, or the clear and consistent resistance to the aims of global capitalism by the anti-APEC protesters.

It becomes quite clear just whose interests the press represents when these events are investigated as the public representation of an ongoing class conflict. The erasure is both amusing and amazing. A survey of historical writing on Vancouver demonstrates just how thoroughly class conflicts are ignored. When the Industrial Workers of the World or "Wobblies" are even mentioned, it is often as an aside, and in Chuck Davis' *Vancouver Book* (the supposed reference of record for all things Vancouver), they are referred to as and reduced to the "International Workers of the World"—at best a laughable redundancy. I have come to believe that these omissions and errors are not merely accidental, but the result of a deliberate, yet unthinking, ideological conspiracy to demean and deny working-class history because it is the only meaningful threat to the dominant program. It is far too easy to dismiss the anarcho-syndicalism of the Wobblies, or the socialism of the Mothers Against Capitalism, or the anarchist leanings of hippies lighting up in Gastown, or the students protesting global capitalism and organizations such as APEC, as the ravings of a lunatic fringe. In whose interest is it to view these events as ongoing battles in a class war against the excesses of capitalism? On the other hand, in whose interest is it to paint a picture of the smooth ascent to dominance of a free market capitalist economic system unchallenged and therefore unfettered by any opposition, or even criticism? Is it any wonder the electoral political spectrum is so narrow and narrowly reported? Democracy and capitalism are not necessarily twin bedfellows. There is a clear agenda to divide the working class against itself, and to perpetuate the myth that the class war is over, that there is nothing left to fight for. As Michael Campbell, *Vancouver Sun* financial columnist, pointed out in a column on globalism, "it is not our job to question the new global economy, but to figure out how we can benefit."

While the worker has only his or her labour, capital has at its disposal the "free" press, the "independent" judiciary, and the "democratic" legislature to bargain with in their relentless war for profit. One wonders if employers will only be happy when workers are nothing more than wage slaves, totally responsible for their own well being. "Remember there is only one taxpayer," we are constantly reminded, implying that corporations don't, or at least shouldn't, contribute anything more than jobs. If riots are the symptom, capitalism is the disease.

The rhetoric of class politics has never been completely subsumed in the discourse of the people of the province of B.C., as much as the editorial writers in *The Vancouver Sun* might wish it to be. As long as capital continues to prove itself incapable of meaningful reform, riots will continue to be a part of the ongoing class war, and Vancouver will continue to be a vital site in the ongoing struggle.

CHAPTER 1

Anti-Asian Riots
September 7-9, 1907

TROUBLE IN CHINATOWN
BY W.R. GORDON

There's trouble down in Chinatown and the Chinks are spitting blue
The cops have yanked old Tai Kee's bank and all his layout, too.
The fan-tan game and the py-gow frame and the chuck-luck mat all went
In one fell swoop when Sergeant Troop and his "bulls" collected rent.

The games were going with a handsome showing and noisy, smoky hum,
While thoughts of raids and police parades were far from the yellow scum.
The Air was thick as burnt clay brick; the smoke you could cut in chunks,
But the monks were gay in their saffron way as they bet their hard-earned plunks

A swell young Chink in a jacket pink lounged by the outer door.
His eyes were closed and you'd swear he dozed, but he saw a whole lot more
than you or I, if we passed by, would take in at a look,
For he was scout for the whole layout and the street was his lesson book.

A cop walked by and the Chink's slant eye read trouble as he passed,
And before another could follow the other that outer door slammed fast.
He pulled a string, and, funny thing, two more banged down the hall,
While in the room the noisy hum had changed to a heathenish bawl.

But the cops were wise; they had used their eyes to size up Tai Kee's joint.
They went at the wall in the dark back hall with an axe and crowbar point.
In a minute or two they laid plain to view the murky gambling den;
They swarmed inside and the way they tied those Chinks was worth a ten.

Five at a time in a jabbering line, they knotted them queue to queue,
While the "muck-a-hai's" and "mo-bing-ka–tai's" turned the place an indigo blue
There were forty odd, too heavy a load for the "Black Maria" van,
So some had to walk for a block, pig-tailed like a human fan.

Now that is why the big ki-yi is heard in Chinatown.
The row they'll raise will be heard all ways round the streets that they hold down;
But it's all in the game, it's ever the same; they're raided from day to day.
When work is slack the cops fall back on the Chinks for a grandstand play.

[FROM BRITISH COLUMBIA MAGAZINE, SEPTEMBER 1911.]

Boarded shop windows in Chinatown after the 1907 Anti-Asian Riot.
PHILIP TIMMS PHOTO,
VANCOUVER PUBLIC LIBRARY, SPECIAL COLLECTIONS, VPL 939

VANCOUVER'S FIRST MUNICIPAL election in May of 1886 was an early opportunity to show exactly what the new city stood for. Hastings Mill manager R.H. Alexander had brought sixty millworkers to the polls to cast their vote for him as a mayoral candidate. Unfortunately for him—and for them—the men were Chinese and the statute incorporating the city of Vancouver denied the vote to both Chinese and Indian. The sixty Chinese males were driven from the polls with fists and clubs, all the way back to the mill. It seems the only reason this was not considered the city's first riot is because there was no property damage, and the police were not called: no damage, no police; no charges, no riot.

This vigilante enforcement of the city charter was not enough for many Vancouverites. The great fire of June 1886 presented another opportunity, as Chinese-owned buildings and residences had been burned out along with almost everyone else (the difference being that resolutions were passed to prevent the Chinese from rebuilding). Soon, The Knights of Labour organized a boycott of all Vancouver businesses that employed, sold food to, or in any way served Chinese residents. A black cross was painted on the sidewalk in front of any store that did not participate in the boycott. Businesses were intimidated into firing Chinese and hiring whites. Funds were made available to any Chinese willing to leave the city. A company was formed to buy out Chinese businesses, and some Chinese workers were simply taken to the docks and put on the steamer to Victoria, "back to where they came from."

Some employers, notably labour contractor Lew Shew, took legal action against the mayor, an alderman, and others on citizens' committees. He sued for the damage caused when they attempted to run him out of town. He lost the first round, but a short time later, with John McDougall or "McDougall Chinee" as he was known, he won a partial victory, obtaining an injunction from the Supreme Court to prevent similar actions in the future.

McDougall was determined to complete his contract using Chinese labour to clear the Brighouse Estates in Vancouver's West End, despite the continued cross-painting and other efforts to prevent Chinese from taking up residence within the city limits. On February 24, 1887, some three hundred angry men raced from a packed public meeting at City Hall to the camps of the Chinese workers at Coal Harbour. The meeting was the latest in a series of public gatherings intended to solve the Chinese "problem," but these men had their own solution, and met no resistance from either the police or the Chinese labourers when they knocked down and burned shanties, then threw bedding, clothing, and provisions on the fires. Twenty-five workers were beaten at that location and then a smaller mob burnt the homes of ninety Chinese on Carrall Street. The next day, the Chinese negotiated a peace treaty of sorts, allowing one Chinese person to be left in charge of each store; the rest were rounded up and transported to New Westminster. Three rioters, a logger, a milkman and clerk were arrested but later discharged for lack of evidence by Magistrate Blake, a member of one of the many citizen's committees struck to bring about the removal of the Chinese from the city.

B.C.'s Attorney General quickly drafted "A Bill to Preserve the Peace in Vancouver," which passed through all three readings in one day, effectively suspending the city's charter and neutering any and all judicial powers. To add injury to this insult on Vancouver's standing, forty Special Constables were dispatched from Victoria to prevent what was seen to be a descent into mob rule.

For the next twenty years, Vancouver City Council, along with the provincial and federal governments alike, carried out what can only be described as an anti-Asiatic vendetta, including head taxes, which climbed from fifty to one hundred dollars, to five hundred dollars in 1904. These actions were complicated only slightly by their own laws and treaties, such as the Anglo-Japanese Treaty of Commerce and Navigation, ratified by the Dominion of Canada in July 1906, which allowed free movement of goods and citizens. There were also the so-called gentleman's agreements, between Imperial powers Japan and England, acting for Canada in international matters.

A depressed local economy led to high unemployment throughout the summer and fall. Winter was looking no better. In July, over eleven hundred Japanese and Chinese immigrants from Hawaii had arrived aboard a single ship, the Kumeric. Part of the reason for this immigration

Boarded shop windows in Chinatown after the 1907 Anti-Asian Riot.
PHILIP TIMMS PHOTO,
VANCOUVER PUBLIC LIBRARY, SPECIAL COLLECTIONS, VPL 940

of Japanese from Hawaii was an outbreak of bubonic plague on the Islands. This latest in a series of migrant arrivals, to fulfill labour supply contracts between the Nippon Supply Company and the Canadian Pacific Railway, strained the private resources of the city's business community to the point where the Japanese Consul appealed to civic officials to arrange safe transportation for the labourers from the docks to their jobs.

The Province of British Columbia's Immigration Act of 1907 had not been given Royal Assent by the Lieutenant Governor, mainly because it violated international treaties with Japan. Attorney General Bowser, who had drawn up the Act, also happened to be the lawyer for the Nippon Supply Company and was responsible for drawing up the company's contracts to supply Asiatic labour; thus, Bowser profited from the contracting of the labour he publicly pledged to exclude from the province. This double standard also allowed the contracted labour to be paid at about half the going rate of other workers.

Damage done by the Asiatic Exclusion League to the boarding houses of T. Kato and H. Hayashi, 230 and 236 Powell Street.
LIBRARY AND ARCHIVES CANADA / C-023557

On August 12, 1907, Vancouver founded its very own Asiatic Exclusion League, modelled on those in San Francisco and Seattle. In all three cities, labour and organized religion provided the financial and organizational support. In the case of Vancouver, the Knights of Labour were the main sponsoring organization, with active participation from most Christian churches.

Labour Day weekend of 1907 was unusually hot, and several related events conspired to raise temperatures even higher, to the point where scapegoats were needed. Who better to point the finger at than immigrants with little or no voice in the community?

A parade and mass meeting was planned for Saturday September 7, to be sponsored by the Vancouver Asiatic Exclusion League. This demonstration was being held to protest the continuing immigration and the very presence of Japanese, Chinese, and Hindus. It was expected to be the largest ever held, drawing on the participation of trade unions, fraternal organizations, religious groups, veteran's groups, and like-minded citizens. Speakers included politicians, both local and U.S. labour leaders, and religious leaders.

On the Thursday before the demonstration, The Bellingham Massacre of Hindu sawmill workers took place. Five hundred of those who weren't badly injured or hospitalized were force-marched north to the Canadian border, where they had to be allowed to cross because they were British Subjects. A persistent rumour that a boatload of four hundred immigrants was to arrive at the city's docks on the weekend also added fuel to the fire.

On Saturday, parade marshal Major E. Browne began the march from the Cambie Grounds, followed by carriages carrying the Asiatic Exclusion League officials and their friends, families, invited speakers, three marching bands, and an estimated five thousand people on foot—many waving small white banners reading "For A White Canada." They headed west on Georgia, north on Granville and east on Hastings to Westminster Avenue (now Main Street) to City Hall, one building south of the intersection of what is now Main and Hastings. Banners lined the route proclaiming the danger to the White Man's security posed by the Asiatic presence. An effigy of the Lieutenant Governor, along with a sign announcing its burning at City Hall, was paraded. The likeness may not have been recognizable, but the name of Robert Dunsmuir, the Queen's representative who would not proclaim the Immigration Act, (also a very wealthy capitalist who profitted from Asiatic labour in his Vancouver Island mines) would have drawn instant negative reaction.

The City Hall, which Mayor Bethune, a devoted member of the Asiatic Exclusion League, had allowed for the use of the group held only a fraction of the crowd, and while the speeches were being delivered—four by men of the cloth—the dummy was set on fire outside. A resolution, calling on the federal government to allow the B.C. Immigration Act, and calling for the passage of a Federal Act to perpetually exclude Asiatics from the country of Canada as a whole, was passed. While the effigy was still burning, A. E. Fowler, secretary of the Seattle Japanese and Corean (sic) Exclusion League, came out onto the steps and whipped the crowd into a frenzy.

City Hall was conveniently located halfway between Chinatown and Japantown. First the crowd marched a couple of blocks to Chinatown. Reports claim a young boy broke the first window with a well-thrown rock. The crowd joined in and threw bricks and rocks until every piece of

Damage done by the Asiatic Exclusion League to the store of K. Okada, 201 Powell Street.
LIBRARY AND ARCHIVES CANADA / C-023555

glass in the area lay shattered in the streets. The surprised Chinese could only lock their doors and set up barricades to protect themselves. At this point, Asians, including some of the Bellingham refugees, were apparently moving freely in the crowd. The animosity of the crowd seemed more symbolic than personal. Property damage was heavy, but few, if any, physical injuries were reported. The crowd soon remembered that their main target was the Japanese, so they regrouped on Westminster Avenue at Powell, the entry to what was known as "little Yokohama." The Japanese-owned drygoods store on the southeast corner was the first target of the thousand-strong mob, inflicting $2,400 in damages to the building and merchandise with a steady barrage of stones and bricks.

By ten o'clock, the badly outnumbered police force, which had called in all off-duty officers from the total force of about two dozen, was unable to have any effect, and their safety was often in doubt. The fire brigade was also called in to help. Arrests were few, in part because the crowd would rescue anyone captured; a bookkeeper, an Italian labourer, and a newly arrived Dane were among the very few who were actually held and charged with rioting.

Shortly after the rioters turned onto Powell Street, they met with well-armed resistance from the Japanese community. In addition to hand-to-hand combat with clubs, knives and guns, rocks, bricks, bottles, and blocks of wood were thrown from the roofs of buildings. The rioters made it as far as The Powell Street Grounds (now Oppenheimer Park), fighting a pitched man-to-man battle every step of the way. The unexpected resistance and high number of casualties caused the large mob to disperse without further large-scale incidents.

Both Chinatown and Japantown were soon behind police street barricades, but different factions of the mob continued their destructive ways well into Monday night when the Japanese Language School on Alexander Street was set on fire at about eight-thirty. One report set the number of arrests at twenty-four with only one case being heard, noting that the procedure was a joke; another claimed that eighteen were arrested Saturday night, and five on Sunday, for a total of twenty-three, commenting that "those with political friends were few." The only conviction seems to have been the bookkeeper for the North Vancouver Ferry Company who was fined fifty dollars for assaulting a police sergeant.

The largest impact in Vancouver was the withdrawal of labour by the Chinese and Japanese. All Chinese workers went on strike, and the Japanese held a mass meeting at the Powell Street Grounds Monday afternoon to consider their actions. Thanks mainly to high-level diplomacy from Great Britain under pressure from their ally Japan, more serious redress was to come in the form of Royal Commissions to be undertaken by William Lyon Mackenzie King, at that time the federal Deputy Minister of Labour. One each for the settlement of Japanese and Chinese losses during the riots, and another inquiry into the immigration of Oriental labourers to Canada.

The commission into Japanese losses sat for eleven days at Pender Hall and recommended awards totalling $9,036, including legal expenses and a recommendation that the Japanese Consulate be paid $1,600 for expenses, which the Consul refused. It is useful to note that of the 107

Royal Commission Reports

claims made, businesses represented included one bank, five barber shops, two bath houses, seven candy stores, four employment offices, thirteen general stores, one hatter's shop, nine hotels, one newspaper, one restaurant, one rice mill, two shoemakers, and one watchmaker. The Chinese commission was similar except for the claims of a couple of opium factories which were not honoured, and led King to later push for the outlawing of the drug. No claims for weapons or ammunition were allowed, although many of the defenders had to purchase guns and ammunition for their own protection. Significantly, neither the riots nor their causes were discussed in either of the reports.

It must be remembered, and the accompanying lists makes it clear, that within the Chinese and Japanese communities, capitalism was in full flower. The fruit of that system is what was attacked. Admittedly, it was the property of Japanese and Chinese capitalists that was destroyed. However that could only benefit the white capitalists. In no way would it further the cause of workers. The capitalists who were firmly in control of all institutions had no intention of excluding the very workers who allowed them to turn a handsome profit on their investment. The riot and similar racially motivated incidents did, however, allow them to separate workers by race and thus rate of pay, which served only to depress the wage rates of all workers. Duped again.

In the main, public opinion seemed to be that the sentiments that sparked the riots were quite reasonable and sensible, even god-given in that the white and yellow race could never live together and that North America was meant for the white race. Nevertheless, the violence of the outbreak was unacceptable. Certainly, the Asiatic Exclusion League was not deterred in the least, and they continued to press for the complete exclusion of all Asiatics. This does not mean that other races or ethnic groups were not targeted; it is simply to suggest that their visibility made them an easy target.

The question remains: If it was demonstrable that whites and Asiatics could not coexist, why were Asiatics allowed into the country in the first place? Why was there a treaty allowing freedom of movement for at least the Japanese? Why were Hindus allowed membership in, and the

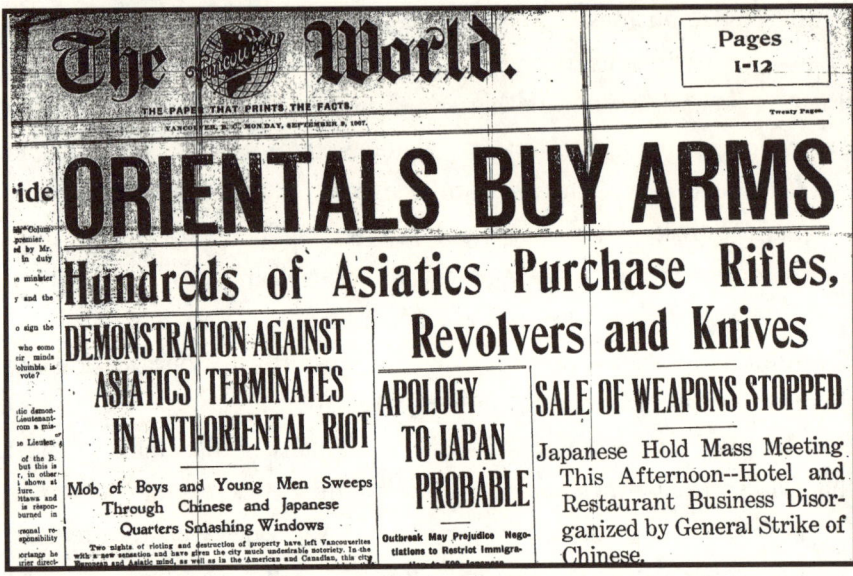

Front Page, *The Vancouver World*, 1907.

protection of, the British Empire? Few if any of these immigrants came to Canada illegally; they were, in the main, brought into the country to fulfil labour contracts with large employers such as the CPR and Wellington Collieries (owned by Dunsmuir). Their labour had little or no effect on the work or wages of others, yet when they banded together for their own protection they were criticized for their inability to integrate. When some accepted unfair wages and conditions rather than rebel, they were criticized. When others competed or resisted, they were seen as a threat.

This selective and collective anxiety seems to be the product of manipulation by economic powers situated far outside the realm of the local Vancouver politic. Cheap (Oriental) labour was needed to build the country, and international trade with Japan and China and India was imperative to maintain profits for traders and bankers alike. Japan needed labour and soldiers for both their industrial and imperial adventures, so happily agreed to limit emigration. The tacit "gentlemen's" agreements were not broken, but still the populace of Vancouver were in a frenzy of opposition to practices that were both legal and deemed necessary by the elites that profited from them. A good rule of thumb seemed to be, follow the money and see where it meets politics.

This is a classic case of the capitalist system using its political, judicial, and religious components to manipulate labour into doing their dirty work. In this case, labour was only too willing to act in the interest of capital and against the workers' best interests. Capitalists such as Dunsmuir, who was also the lieutenant governor, (represented in the political sphere by the Attorney General Bowser) needed Oriental labour because it was more "productive," i.e., cheap and expendable. They also needed to maintain trade relations with Japan and China. Capital has one overriding concern, and that is profit. If the major cost of doing business is labour then it would be prudent to limit the cost of labour. What better way to limit labour costs than to bring in a group of people who could then be denied all rights and privileges based on their race? At the same time they could act as a restraint on the wages of "citizen" employees. Further, if the citizens—read: high-wage employees—could contain the "immigrant" employees through social controls, which cost the capitalists nothing, then profits would be maximized. The "Japs" and "Chinks" do the heavy work, the whites supervise or manage to keep them in their place. It's called wage slavery for a reason.

The Asiatic Exclusion League was nothing more than a front for the Knights of Labour, an early conservative labour formation, more interested in cutting deals with bosses than acting in the interest of member workers. Their American leadership pushed for the exclusion of all Orientals on the premise that whites and Orientals could not live together and every incident they managed to provoke was further evidence. Many workers shared these racist attitudes, but many did not. The IWW, known as the Wobblies, and founded in 1905 as an offshoot of the Western Federation of Miners, believed that racism was just one tool in the arsenal of the bosses. An injury to one is an injury to all. The Wobblies preferred to stand on the picket line with Chinese and Japanese workers for the benefit of all workers. If you helped to hold down the wages of one worker, you were, by logical extension, holding back your own wages. The employer could thereby always find someone to work for less. The Wobblies had a deep and long-standing distrust of the institutions and personalities of capitalism based on historical precedent. Their instinct was to be against everything that capitalism was in favour of. They weren't too often wrong. Unfortunately, their voices were not heard at this critical time in Vancouver.

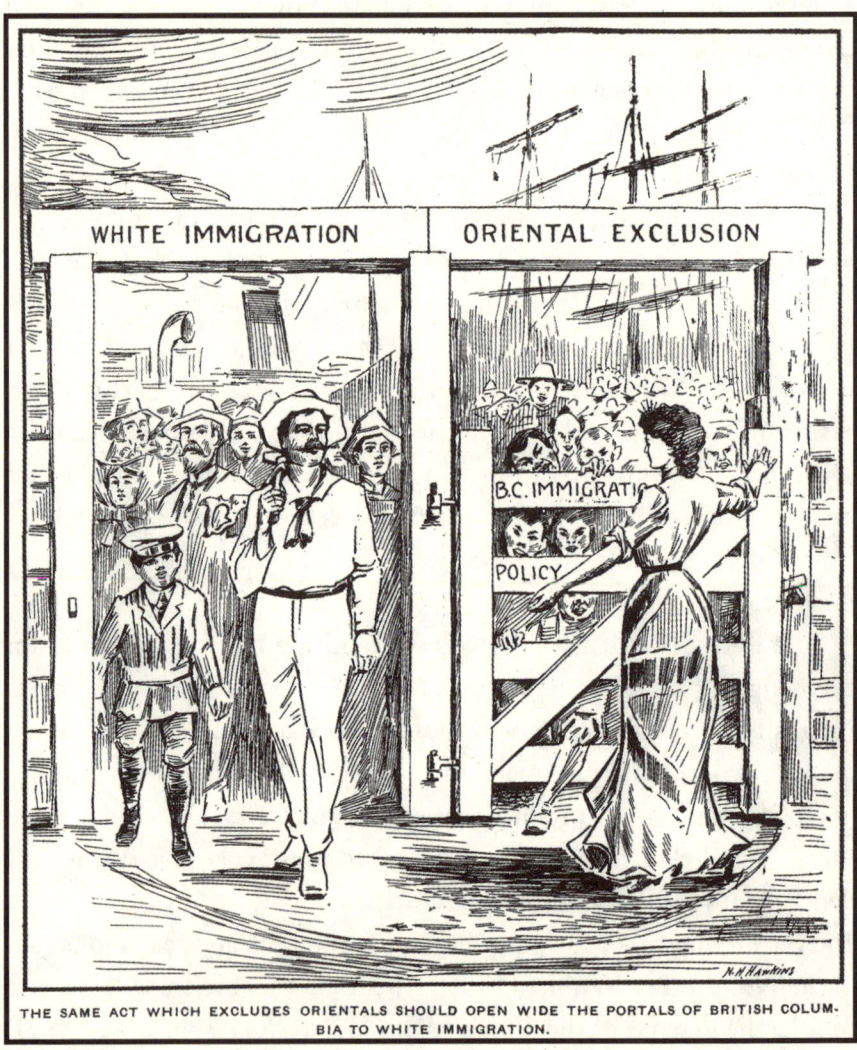

THE SAME ACT WHICH EXCLUDES ORIENTALS SHOULD OPEN WIDE THE PORTALS OF BRITISH COLUMBIA TO WHITE IMMIGRATION.

VANCOUVER PUBLIC LIBRARY, SPECIAL COLLECTIONS, VPL 39046

JAP RIOT, MAY 13, 1942

What I was afraid of was a riot like in 1907, but worse. Because anti-Japanese feeling was much higher than ever before. I thought that if we did anything to provoke trouble something really horrible would happen. We could all get massacred, women and children too.

—RYUICHI YOSHIDA,
A Man of Our Times:
The Life-history of a Japanese-Canadian Fisherman

IN THE LONG tradition of Vancouver riots there is one that is unclassifiable, mainly because it cuts across so many lines and fits so many categories. At once a race riot, this time it was also a victims-of-racism riot, a prison riot, a food riot, a political riot, and a *language* riot. The Canadian government moved quickly after the attack on Pearl Harbour in December of 1941. By May of the following year, many of British Columbia's citizens of Japanese extraction had already been moved beyond the hundred-mile exclusion zone. Japanese property was being seized and sold to pay for the costs of the actions against them. Long simmering anti-Asian—and specifically anti-Japanese—sentiments were running high. Politicians were pledging to deal with the "Jap" problem once and for all, through forced dispersal within Canada and deportation. The Japanese community was faced with an impossible dilemma—in order to prove their loyalty to Canada they had to submit to draconian measures. There were no trials, secret or otherwise. Government bureaucrats, under the direction of politicians, acted out the worst fears of any minority, by violating local, national, and international laws based solely on race in the name of national security. Japanese born in Canada were declared enemy aliens because of nothing more than their race, while Canadians of German and Italian extraction had little to fear from the government of Canada. Language is at the root of this riot: official, state-sanctioned, socially acceptable racist language.

The front page of *The Vancouver Sun* of Thursday, May 14 of 1942 contained an article with the headline "Japanese will be interned" under

> **JAPS CLEAN UP MESS THEY MADE IN RIOT**
>
> While vigilant guards kept watch on them a group of Japanese were put to work today cleaning up the mess they made when they heaved paper and broken furniture through the windows of the Immigration Building Wednesday. Gathered at the windows above another group of Japs shouted encouragement at their comrades who are sweeping up the mess. A number of cardboard cartons were filled with the refuse.

JAP RIOT: Vancouver Immigration Sheds, *Vancouver Province*.

the cut-line "riot sequel" and the subhead "military guards patrol scene of ruckus," concerning an incident at the Immigration Building at the foot of Burrard Street. Some of the other front page stories were headlined "Chinese Cut Jap Lines in Burma," "Allied Planes Smash at Japs Amboina Base," "Nazis say Japs Are Big Liars." The front-page article is continued inside with the headline, "Jap Riot." *The Province* headline reads, "Japs in City Rioting Will Be Interned" under the cut-line "Statement in House." *The Province* has two pictures, one of the Immigration Building with prisoners hanging out the upper windows and debris on the ground. The other shows a woman with a suitcase waving toward the Immigration Building in the distance with two armed soldiers between her and the building. A long simmering desire in British Columbia to get rid of its citizens of Japanese ancestry had flared up again, and the articles openly display this anti-Asiatic sentiment.

"First reports were that the Japs staged their orgy of Banzai-shouting and wholesale destruction as a protest against an order prohibiting relatives and friends from talking to them through their barred windows." The report continues in bold: "While this order probably touched off the disturbance, *The Vancouver Sun* has learned that the incident comes at the climax of a two-week period of waiting behind bars, during which Ottawa failed to issue orders for removal of the Japs to camps elsewhere in Canada."

The paper also states that the men had refused to report to the B.C. Securities Commission and were "picked up" by the RCMP and turned over to military authorities.

The rioters "smashed furniture, knocked plaster from the walls," turned a fire hose on guards, broke windows, and knocked out the iron gratings while throwing streamers of tissue out the broken windows. While city police watched; "They did keep a growing crowd of white spectators well back," CPR police and soldiers were needed to quell the riot. The paper states that the troops requested but did not use tear gas acquired from city police when the disturbance was resumed in the evening. There is no mention of any gunshots. The B.C. Security Commission Chairman Austin Taylor said, "Some of the Japanese got a little fed up about being kept in the building, and got a little exuberant. There was more yelling than anything else. There was nothing malicious about the trouble, it was more playful than anything else."

What *Sun* readers weren't told is that many of the men being held in the Immigration sheds were Canadian Citizens who had voluntarily surrendered to the B.C. Security Commission to be "evacuated" from the West Coast and "interned" as enemy aliens. On April 25, sixty-seven members of the Nisei mass evacuation group (NMEG) showed up at the gates to the shed to give themselves up for internment as part of the protest against families being split up in the wartime evacuation of Japanese people from protected areas in both the United States and Canada. One significant difference in the two countries was the American provision for family groups to remain together.

Roy Miki, in his book *Redress: Inside the Japanese Call for Justice*, lays out the history of resistance within the Japanese-Canadian community.

The Vancouver Sun

SINCE 1886 VANCOUVER'S MOST USEFUL INSTITUTION

A newspaper devoted to progress and democracy, tolerance and freedom of human thought.

THURSDAY, MAY 14, 1942

Japs Are Poor Sportsmen, Indeed!

Our people have been disposed to overlook small irritations in connection with the Japanese community; little attention has been paid to hunger strikes and similar exhibitions of temporary bad temper. But the incident at the immigration shed yesterday was of much larger calibre and naturally arouses widespread disgust and resentment.

There is no excuse whatever for the wanton rioting staged by many scores of the Japanese detained there. The public will rightly conclude that the outbreak was a manifestation of Nazi ideals which these people have absorbed and now have adopted as their own.

Not a day passes but The Sun receives letters of complaint at the too-soft treatment of the Japanese by the authorities. But our view is that it is better to err on the side of leniency and kind treatment than to allow the Japanese any possible cause of anger or protest. So we have advised our readers that our officials are trying to be patient in a difficult operation. Austin Taylor and his mounted police executives and operatives have leaned over backwards so that no cause or shadow of excuse may ever be given in Hong Kong or Singapore for any reprisal against Canadian or British prisoners. (It happens that an article on this page today throws an important light on this subject.)

The Sun is glad to record that the vast majority of Japanese have accepted with reasonably good grace the excellent arrangements made for their removal from coastal areas. An amazing amount of care and consideration has been expended by officers under instruction from the government to avoid all possible hardships. In fact, the routine of their departure, including examination and enrollment and temporary housing at Hastings Park, could not be better if it had been designed to treat them to a picnic at public expense.

The bulk of the colony accepts everything agreeably and courteously, as a "necessary evil" in their estimation; but especially amongst the Nisei, born in Vancouver and many unfortunately sent back to Japan for an army education, there are a number of bad actors. They hotly declined to accept the very generous terms of the government and there was nothing left but to consign them to internment as suspect aliens.

The Japanese themselves must realize how tactics of this kind make it all the more certain that after the war all people of Japanese extraction in this country will have to go back to their fatherland. Most certainly Canada is not going to be saddled with a hot-headed group of trouble-makers, full of defiance of authority, ready to destroy Canadian institutions and property. It was good news to hear yesterday that fishing boats and B.C. cannery plants have now been fully re-staffed by people replacing the Japanese. There may be temporary shortages of labor in some categories caused by the departure of the Japanese, but readjustments will be made and in a few months their absence will no longer be felt. B.C. has been more than patient tolerating them for nearly half a century with their insolent boring-in and aggressive methods. We certainly won't have them back on any terms at all.

Editorial Page, *Vancouver Sun*, May 14, 1942.

The NMEG was not radical, they would consent to "evacuation" but were resisting the break-up of family groups. They were militant however, and the protests at the immigration sheds were part of an organized resistance and demand for rights and justice. The protest was one part of a resistance "gambaru," which divided the community, but made it clear that the policies of the Canadian government were racially-based and not security-based. The divisions in the community are fictionalized in Joy Kogawa's *Obasan*: "In Petawawa there are one hundred and thirty Nisei interned for rioting and crying *Banzai!*, shaving their heads and carrying 'Hino-maru' flags. Damn fools."

Miki has used a self-published memoir translated from Japanese, written by one of the participants, that tells a much different story from that in *The Vancouver Sun*. According to Robert Katsumasa Okazaki, the men virtually had to force their way into the sheds, which were guarded by bayonet-wielding soldiers, when they reported for evacuation. After being held for more than three weeks in subhuman conditions, their protest was met with armed troops using tear gas and firing bullets into the building where the men were held. The men in the shed were shortly shipped out to internment camps, in clear violation of the Geneva Conventions, which prohibit the detention of a country's own citizens. As Miki points out, they left Vancouver as "detainees," and arrived in Angler and Petawawa, Ontario as "enemy aliens." For the most part these were Canadian citizens who had had their property confiscated and sold and the money was used to pay for their keep in prison camps under brutal conditions. As time goes by, it is likely that more instances of resistance will come to light.

In the same issue of *The Sun*, "A newspaper devoted to progress and Democracy, tolerance and freedom of Human thought," there is an editorial decrying the "wanton rioting" entitled, "Japs are Poor Sportsmen, Indeed!" declaring the "outbreak" at the Immigration sheds to be "a manifestation of Nazi ideals which these people have absorbed and now have adopted as their own."

Arrests at the Free Speech Demonstration, Vancouver, January 18, 1912.
BRITISH COLUMBIA ARCHIVES D-06368

CHAPTER 2

Free Speech Riots 1909 & 1911

The working class and the employing class have nothing in common. There can be no peace so long as hunger and want are found among millions of the working people and the few, who make up the employing class, have all the good things of life. Between these two classes a struggle must go on until the workers of the world organize as a class, take possession of the means of production, abolish the wage system, and live in harmony with the Earth. We find that the centring of the management of industries into fewer and fewer hands makes the trade unions unable to cope with the ever-growing power of the employing class. The trade unions foster a state of affairs which allows one set of workers to be pitted against another set of workers in the same industry, thereby helping defeat one another in wage wars. Moreover, the trade unions aid the employing class to mislead the workers into the belief that the working class have interests in common with their employers.

These conditions can be changed and the interest of the working class upheld only by an organization formed in such a way that all its members in any one industry, or in all industries if necessary, cease work whenever a strike or lockout is on in any department thereof, thus making an injury to one an injury to all. Instead of the conservative motto, "A fair day's wage for a fair day's work," we must inscribe on our banner the revolutionary watchword, "Abolition of the wage system." It is the historic mission of the working class to do away with capitalism. The army of production must be organized, not for everyday struggle with capitalists, but also to carry on production when capitalism shall have been overthrown. By organizing industrially we are forming the structure of the new society within the shell of the old.

[INDUSTRIAL WORKERS OF THE WORLD PREAMBLE TO THE CONSTITUTION]

UNTIL 1872, CANADA treated unions as criminal conspiracies in restraint of trade, as did British Law. Despite harsh sanctions, workers still found it necessary to organize, but unions had to be incredibly strong to withstand the united onslaught of employers, police and courts until the right to organize was enshrined in law and bargaining rights could be enforced. Unionism was just one front in the struggle for human dignity, accomplishing such benefits as Worker's Compensation for injuries or death on the job. It is always good to remember that people died in the fight for the eight-hour day. In the political sphere, advances in social legislation that we have largely taken for granted, but are now under attack again, had to be wrested from the ruling class through years of struggle and confrontation. Unemployment Insurance was introduced in 1940; Family Allowances, 1945; Old Age Security, 1951; Pensions, 1966; and medicare, in 1968. All of these advances, which were essentially compromises on the part of capital with labour in order to maintain their hegemony and privilege, are again on the table, as capitalism globalizes and demands that workers surrender these hard-won victories in the name of competitiveness and productivity. It is also interesting to note that riots virtually disappeared from the scene during the time frame of 1940 to 1968 when it seemed like it might actually be possible to reform capital.

At the beginning of the twentieth century, a scene like this might have played out on a Vancouver street.

> Two men stagger out of an alley near Hastings and Carrall. "Help! Help! I've been robbed!"
>
> One is carrying a soapbox while supporting his dishevelled friend.
>
> "Somebody stole all his capital! Took all the money he ever earned. Everything is gone." They set up their soapbox while the Salvation Army band is playing across the street.
>
> "Gather 'round people and hear his story!" A crowd begins to form on the sidewalk. The men are careful to organize them, leaving room for pedestrians to pass.

The roughest-looking man climbs up on the soapbox and shakes his fist. "I have been robbed, that's right. I've been robbed by capitalism. Every dollar of profit is a dollar stolen from a worker's pocket. I have had the money I made working on the docks taken right out of my pocket by a boss more interested in the health of his bottom line than the well being of me and my family. And that, ladies and gentlemen, is why we are here today breaking your town's law against gathering on the street, even though right across the street in direct contravention of the same anti-loitering law, the Starvation Army is allowed to preach their brand of "pie in the sky when you die liberalism."

"Now that I have your attention I would like to tell you about the fight the Industrial Workers of the World are waging in your town for the freedom to speak in the streets. This is not simply the freedom to make a political speech and ask for your vote. No, we demand the freedom to organize an industrial union of all workers of all races, religion, age and sex. The freedom to advocate the end to a class of people who are responsible for all the misery in the world. The freedom to dump the bosses off our backs."

The worker begins to sing from a little red book.

> *Are you poor forlorn and hungry?*
> *Are there lots of things you lack?*
> *Is your life made up of misery?*
> *Then dump the bosses off your back.*

These words, written by John Brill, were sung to the tune of the well-known hymn "Take it to the Lord in Prayer." Another popular favourite would have been the "Preacher and the Slave," or any other song by Joe Hill, who had wandered the "thousand-mile picket line" from San Diego to British Columbia, writing and singing. Joe Hill might have stood kitty-corner from the Salvation Army at Hastings and Carrall and sung:

> *And the starvation army they play*
> *And they sing and they clap and they pray.*
> *Till they get all your coin on the drum*
> *Then they tell you when you are on the bum:*

CHORUS

> *You will eat, bye and bye,*
> *In that glorious land above the sky;*
> *Work and pray, and live on hay,*
> *You'll get pie in the sky when you die.*

THE INDUSTRIAL WORKERS of the World, or Wobblies', critique of capitalism covered not only economic and social concerns, but extended into the arena of religion, exposing the hypocrisy of preaching obedience to political masters whose very practices violated the teachings of all the major religions. They were not afraid to challenge any authority that stood in the way of their ultimate goal of a cooperative commonwealth, a visionary utopia reliant on the workers for its ultra-democratic process that was in and of itself utopian. Enacting their radical message by organizing around practical issues like the eight-hour day, the IWW came to be viewed with a fear that inspired vindictive and often illegal reactions.

Up and down the West Coast of North America, the basic conditions that led to "free speech fights" were nearly always the same. Civic leaders were nervous about both the language and content of the public speeches given by members of the Industrial Workers of the World. They understood only too well that the IWW was advocating the overthrow of capitalism and the end of privilege. Capitalism was under attack from many quarters, but the capitalists were not about to give up without a fight. The weapons of choice ranged from the legalistic, but largely ineffective, banning of street speaking, which led to full jails and expensive prisoner upkeep. Violence by police, vigilantes, hired goons, militias and the military were stages in the escalation. Somewhere in between, divide-and-conquer strategies were used, a familiar tactic of oppression used by the ruling class to back what they saw as their god-given right to profit at the expense of others.

All the working class had was the right to organize, guaranteed by the protection of free speech. The IWW was determined to make use of their rights to obtain what they saw as their legal ends: the education and organization of the working class to eventually drive capitalism from the face of the earth by eliminating the coercive nature of wage slavery. Elected officials, hearing only threats of violence and what they regarded as blasphemy, pushed by their panicking business constituents, would begin by selectively enforcing hastily drawn bylaws, and the fight would be on.

Invariably, the press would take the side of moderation and decry any perceived attack on the status quo. The IWW were always portrayed as wild-eyed radicals, capable of any outrage. In fact, mere membership in the IWW became a crime near the end of World War II in both Canada and the United States. The Wobblies faced a formidable array of enemies, including elected officials and their well-armed enforcement branches of police, army, and militia; the so-called free press and allied business interests; and the religious element, who were offended by the irreligious nature of the campaign. Even other workers, like labour skates (workers who had signed on to the historical compromise between labour and capital known as unions) and scissorbills (workers lacking in class consciousness) were against the IWW. The Wobblies seized the initiative by characterizing clashes with all of these groups as "free speech" fights. This is just one example of early media manipulation, although free speech was not a universally respected or well-entrenched right at that time.

Conditions leading up to the first free speech fight in Vancouver centred on a fiercely anti-labour mayor and council who refused to implement the eight-hour day for civic workers, despite its being approved by plebiscite, as well as insisting on contracting-out day labour. American real estate developer C.S. Douglas, the newly elected mayor, also initiated a "clean-up the streets" campaign directed primarily against radicals from Seattle, a city which was "cleaning up" its own streets in preparation for the upcoming Alaska-Yukon-Pacific exposition. In one day in April, nineteen of these "undesirables" were prevented from disembarking from the Seattle ferry. Vagrancy charges climbed. A long and bitter IWW-led longshoreman's strike against the CPR had just been broken by the use of scabs, and the cost of living was on the rise again.

Carrall Street, between Hastings and Cordova, had long been the best place for street speakers. In the centre of the worker's community, with many labour organizations headquartered in the immediate area, there was always a guaranteed audience. In fact, the Salvation Army had its usual spot covered on the other side of Hastings Street.

On Sunday, April 4, 1909, Vancouver city police asked the IWW and Socialist Party of Canada speakers to disperse, and when they refused, issued summonses. Missing the point of free speech entirely, the police contended the streets were for walking on and the speakers could simply hire a hall to get their message out. Tellingly, the Salvation Army was allowed to proceed with their larger, noisier, and more disruptive street meeting.

On April 6, as the trial of the men was adjourned for a week, the judge offered that the men should refrain from further public speaking. Of course, another meeting had already been scheduled for the same location on the very next night. The Vancouver Trades and Labour Council organized a rally in front of City Hall, at which they extended sympathy and pledged support.

The battle continued both in the court and on the streets. The first of May saw another mass meeting in front of City Hall, where as *The Province* put it, "There were several speakers, who advocated most strongly the principles and ideas of the revolutionists." On May 13, Lucy Parsons, IWW member and widow of Haymarket martyr Albert Parsons, outlined the circumstances of the unjust murder of her husband by the authorities to a large crowd, and William Taylor, who had been fined for his original speech, addressed the crowd against the magistrate's orders, demanding that free speech be restored. More street meetings and more arrests followed. Those who were not arrested helped raise money for the imprisoned.

On May 18, more than a thousand people gathered at Hastings and Carrall. When the speaker refused to give the police his name, the four constables and a sergeant moved off. The next night, the police observed but did not disrupt the speeches and the stand-off was over. Open police harassment stopped, the crown did not prosecute the remaining cases with any vigour, and the IWW could declare a victory for free speech even though the solidarity of the working class on the issue was at best questionable.

During the Victoria Free Speech Fight of 1911, the radicals opposed the city official's decree: that unionists, Wobblies, and socialists could only speak on one out-of-the-way corner, while the religionists went unimpeded. As usual, when faced with fines or jail time, the Wobblies chose jail, and the streets were filled with protesters demanding that the labour speakers be accorded at least equal treatment to the Salvation Army. Their demands were met in that all street speaking was restricted to certain corners, but at least no one group was denied equal treatment. In the end, seven Wobblies chose to have their fines remain in the hands of the workers, stating, "We have freedom of speech, the food and lodging and the fines stowed away in our jeans. What did you get out of it Mr. Boss?"

Free Speech Demonstration, Vancouver, January 18, 1912.
BRITISH COLUMBIA ARCHIVES C-05634

EVENTUALLY, THE FREE speech fights would turn from skirmishes to outright riots. By 1912, the downturn in the pre-war economic boom led to high levels of unemployment. Workers gravitated to the city, encouraged by the Salvation Army, government officials, and the usual civic "boosters," all of whom had a vested interest in ensuring a large supply of cheap labour eager for the few available jobs. The primitive forms of "workfare" organized by the city were totally inadequate. The IWW continued to hold street meetings to organize the unemployed. The inevitable crackdown on vagrants and transients was soon to follow. Vagrants, by definition, were the poor and unemployed, but the charge itself was a familiar catch-all, used against radicals and organizers under the category of "undesirables."

As street protests continued to escalate, the electorate voted in James Findlay, a law-and-order conservative candidate, as mayor, and city council promptly passed a bylaw banning all outdoor meetings. On January 20, 1912, four men were arrested at an IWW-organized meeting at Cordova and Carrall. Three were charged with vagrancy and the other with assaulting a police officer. The following day, six speakers were

Mayor Findlay's Proclamation

No more remarkable public document than the following proclamation by Mayor Findlay has been offered to the inspection of the community within our recollection:

"TO THE CITIZENS OF VANCOUVER:

"All citizens and other persons who may, out of curiosity or otherwise, join or gather or be near any crowd, mob or assembly, which the police of the city are endeavoring to break up and disperse, are hereby notified and requested to disperse and go away to their homes or places of business immediately upon the police endeavoring to disperse or break up any such crowd, mob or assembly or notifying same to disperse or break up.

"In dispersing and breaking up any such crowd, mob or assembly, it is impossible for the police to distinguish or discriminate between those who form same, so that otherwise innocent and reputable citizens are liable to suffer.

"JAMES FINDLAY,
"Mayor.

"City Hall, January 29, 1912."

Vancouver Province, January 29, 1912.

arrested at Powell and Carrall. On Sunday, January 28, a crowd of several thousand gathered at the Powell Street Grounds to hear Parmeter (Parm) Pettipiece of the Socialist Party of Canada report on his meeting with the provincial government and their response to the current levels of unemployment. The deputy chief of police declared the meeting illegal, and arrested the main speaker. When the crowd protested, he signalled his officers to charge, swinging clubs and horsewhips.

> *"... those not fortunate enough to get out of the way went down like ten-pins before the irresistible onslaught of the officers... The Powell Street Grounds looked something like a battlefield."*
> —*Vancouver Province*, January 29, 1912

Almost thirty arrests were made with bail set at five hundred dollars. The border was sealed to prevent an anticipated Wobbly invasion, and the Interurban rail line was monitored.

What had been expected to prove a diversion from the usual quiet Sunday afternoon routine was fast dwindling into a very poor show. Then something happened. Arthur Wong, member of the Young Chinese society, attired in a natty serge, boutonniere of Chinese lilies, standing collar, and all the accessories of correct dress, from his closely clipped hirsute to his faultless patent leathers, mounted the rostrum amid thunderous applause. Wong was a socialist, and the date might be set down in history as the first wherein one of his race has mounted the open air rostrum. While Wong was "long" on enthusiasm he was woefully "short" on English. However, his elucidation of the socialistic problems was fully as erudite as that of his Christian brothers. Wong's message read something like this.

ANGLO-CHINESE TREAT

"When Manchu him lun China, come 'long like big p'licemans, big club, say 'skidoo,' Chinaman him scatter likee lat before cat; when big p'liceman him come this place two Sunday ago, and I gettee crack on head. Today we no scatter likee chicken. I bin all over world; I see China, Gleat Blittin, alle same. Young Chinese society all bin socialists. I bin reporter China newspaper. I tell em all we no scatter likee chicken when p'liceman come." His explanation of the modus operandi of socialistic acquisition of all wealth and the relegation of the capitalist to the realms of Beelzebub was equally as lucid as the above.

—*Vancouver Province*

Further meetings were broken up by police, including one in Stanley Park, where the speakers used megaphones to address the crowd from boats. The strong current prevented the speakers from being heard and they were arrested when they came ashore. When the IWW upped the ante, hinting at a general strike and sabotage, the other labour groups backed down and compromised with the city in order to pursue electoral reform at the ballot box in the upcoming provincial elections, selling out

Free Speech Demonstration, Vancouver, February 3, 1912.
BRITISH COLUMBIA ARCHIVES C-05634

the Wobs along the way. No meetings were to be allowed on public streets, but public squares could be used. All charges would be dropped. After much wrangling and infighting between labour, civic officials, and the province, limited free speech was reinstated; however, the charges were not dropped and the prisoners, mainly Wobblies, were not released.

> *The entire organization supports Vancouver Workers in their efforts to maintain free speech. The rights of the members of this organization will be enforced in spite of all the corporation lice holding political jobs in the Dominion of Canada. Free speech will be established and maintained in Vancouver, if it takes twenty years. Hold you personally responsible for any injury inflicted upon members of this organization by Cossacks under your control.*
>
> [TELEGRAM FROM VINCENT ST. JOHN, IWW GENERAL SECRETARY TO VANCOUVER MAYOR FINDLAY, FEBRUARY 12-13, 1912.]

Front Page: *The Vancouver World*, February, 1912.

Mainly by publicizing the threat in this letter, the Wobblies were discredited and isolated by their more moderate allies. The argument seemed to be that direct action (i.e. street protest) inevitably led to violence, never mind that the violence could almost always be characterized as a "police riot" and that violence against a vastly better supplied enemy was suicidal. The radical underpinnings of the IWW were repudiated, although further IWW protests took place; soon, more important battles took precedence—for example, the Lawrence textile workers' strike and the San Diego free speech fight.

Without immediate and tangible repression, the IWW could not compete with other more moderate organizations who could deliver small victories at the ballot box and compromises with capital such as welfare, medicare, Pensions and Unemployment Insurance. But whenever capitalist repression of the working class reaches intolerable levels, Wobblies promise that the socialist ideas of the Industrial Workers of the World will answer the call.

CHAPTER 3

Bloody Sunday:
Unemployment Riots of
1935 & 1938

BREAD AND ROSES
As we go marching, marching we battle too for men,
For they are women's children and we mother them again.
Our lives shall not be sweated from birth until life closes.
Hearts starve as well as bodies; give us bread but give us roses.

Unidentified official beating back a group of people, some of whom are shielding their faces, during a demonstration at the Vancouver Post Office.
LIBRARY AND ARCHIVES CANADA / C-020596

Government Hospitality No. 2: unidentified man on a cot in an office.
LIBRARY AND ARCHIVES CANADA / C-020594

> "... If the right to strike is suppressed, or seriously limited, the trade union movement becomes nothing more than one institution among many in the service of capitalism..."
>
> —PIERRE ELLIOT TRUDEAU
> quoted in *Never Say Die* by JOHN STANTON

THE DIRTY THIRTIES were said to have been harder on Vancouver than any other city in Canada. When the boom of the Twenties came to an abrupt end on that "Black Friday" in October of 1929, very few recognized that this was anything more than a temporary setback. Proposed city spending for the year 1930 was $25 million, equal to the provincial budget as Mayor Malkin liked to boast. What Malkin was less inclined to mention was the tripling of the city's relief rolls, a raid by the unemployed on the relief office, downtown streets clogged with protest marches, and the all-too-common arrest and imprisonment of the homeless.

By 1932, thirty-four thousand of a population of a quarter million people were on relief in the city and the annual bill had risen to $2.39 million. Many individuals were hard hit, but it was the business community that panicked. The soon-to-be-infamous Kidd Committee Report, a response to the crisis pressed on the Provincial Government by the Vancouver Board of Trade, the Retail Merchants Association and five Vancouver service clubs, demanded that the provincial budget be slashed from twenty-five to six million, that university funds be cut, that the PGE railroad be abandoned and people be cut off relief completely while remaining social services be greatly reduced. Among the sponsors of the Kidd Committee Report, presumably, were what remained of the city's "eighty-three millionaires" that Premier Duff Patullo had criticized in 1929 for their lack of civic spirit, having never made a single donation to the university or sponsored any major civic enterprise.

These would have been many of the same men who the Shipping Federation's "reorganization committee" invited to a private luncheon in the dining room of the Vancouver Club on April 18, 1935. The Citizen's League was born out of this meeting of the "Committee of 66." Some of the names will be instantly recognizable: VanDusen, Spencer, Woodward, Rogers, Buckerfield, Bell-Irving, Malkin and on and on, a roll call of Vancouver's business leaders led by then-Mayor Gerald G. McGeer, who appointed Brigadier Victor M. Odlum as the front man for this vigilante-style organization. With the addition of Colonel C.E. Edgett and the president of the Shipping Federation J.E. Hall and their frontman/mouthpiece, broadcaster Tom McInnes (who made no distinction of any kind between unions and communists), this was a powerful, moneyed organization fiercely dedicated to the eradication of unions, prepared to use any and all means at their disposal. A campaign, including full-page ads in the daily press attacking the "Bolshevik menace" was only the beginning of their pogrom.

Anti-police demonstration during the Great Depression.
LIBRARY AND ARCHIVES CANADA / C-027899

Hut News, Relief Camp, Harrison Mills, 1932.
VANCOUVER PUBLIC LIBRARY, SPECIAL COLLECTIONS, VPL 8833

As the world economy levelled off in late 1934 and early 1935, the fortunes of the City of Vancouver and its business community improved slightly; however, there was little change for workers, unemployed or otherwise. The federal government's answer to the Great Depression in 1932 was to create a series of "relief camps" across the country. Administered by the Department of National Defence, the camps were hastily erected and often squalid, serving the dual purpose of keeping the young, single men away from urban centres—and any possible protest movements—while providing cheap labour for private industry. Projects were almost always labour intensive, substituting picks, shovels, and wheelbarrows for machinery. The men were paid twenty cents a day. Although no one was forced into the camps, failure to enroll would result in a loss of any relief benefits. Between 1932 and 1936, 170,000 men passed through the camps. Soon enough the camps themselves became the sites of organizing and protest. The Relief Camp Workers' Union, which was affiliated with the Workers' Unity League, organized and began protesting camp conditions, most specifically the militarization of the camps. The leaders of these groups were expelled and subsequently blacklisted, which denied them and their families any form of relief. The men who worked in the relief camps began an organized walk-out. In December of 1934, twelve hundred workers descended on Vancouver and stayed for four weeks, demanding an end to the expulsions and blacklists. In April of 1935, the men in the camps went on strike for "work and wages." Two thousand men, who had been doing heavy labour, left the camps and assembled in Vancouver. Standing on street corners throughout downtown, "tin-canning" to collect money from passers-by—a tactic necessitated by their disqualification from relief—and snarling traffic with near-daily protests, the men could hardly be ignored. Five thousand marched on April 9. Revolution was in the air, at least in the mind of the mayor, Gerry McGeer. After all, by his calendar, it was only eighteen years after the Russian Revolution. The night before reading the Riot Act he would dine on a German naval vessel with representatives of Hitler's government and have an excellent meeting. With over seventy-five thousand registered unemployed in B.C. alone, an uprising seemed inevitable, not just to the politicians but to the capitalists and the workers alike.

> "A STRIKEBREAKER IS A TRAITOR TO HIS GOD, HIS COUNTRY, HIS FAMILY, HIS CLASS!"
> —JACK LONDON, *Portrait of a Scab*

Relief Demonstration.
LIBRARY AND ARCHIVES CANADA / C-079022

A MAJOR DEMONSTRATION was organized by the Relief Camp Worker's Union for April 23. In addition to the now-ubiquitous parade with thousands marching behind brass bands, the organizers had added a new wrinkle. They would take their protests off the street and into a downtown department store. Undercover police infiltrators keeping an eye on the perceived "red menace" were aware of the new tactic, although they did not know which store would be targeted. Police Chief Foster advised his men that the strikers had "mistaken leniency and kindness for timidity" and that stern measures would be necessary if the protest was carried out on private property.

The demonstration began at three o'clock at the Cambie Grounds with the usual speeches by the union leaders and banner-waving and cheering. They marched first to the Kelly, Douglas and Malkin wholesale store in Gastown, entered, walked around and left, causing no damage. They moved next to the Hudson's Bay Company ("Here Before Christ," as it was more popularly known) store where they marched up and down the aisles for about thirty minutes, chanting "Work and Wages." As soon as the police entered to remove the demonstrators, who had refused to leave when asked by the store manager, display cases were smashed and merchandise was thrown at police, but eventually the strikers were driven from the store. Damages were later estimated at five thousand dollars; six policemen were injured and two arrests were made for assaulting a police officer.

The march then continued down Granville Street to Hastings and along Hastings to Victory Square, where more speeches were made and a delegation of ten men was appointed to visit the mayor one block away at City Hall. Mayor McGeer listened to their demands for civic assistance, which of course they were not eligible for because, having no fixed address, they could not provide proof of residence. He not only refused their request, condemning their actions as revolutionary and inexcusable, but also ordered them arrested as they left the building.

When word of the arrests filtered back to the demonstrators, a new delegation was readied to visit City Hall. That was unnecessary because the mayor was on his way to Victory Square, where the crowd had been surrounded on all sides by city police, RCMP and

ARRESTED

Richard Rothery, NFA
George H Wood, 27, NFA
Peter Kennedy, NFA
A. R. Scott, 19 NFA.
John Lawson, 44, 327 East Georgia.
Jim Walsh, 33, NFA.
Mike McCauley, 25, 312 West Georgia.
George Ritchie, 31, 7194 Culloden.
M. Condon, 34, Devon Rooms.
William Davis, 21, 31a West Pender.
Robert Maxwell, 28, 371 Homer.
David Levis, 27, NFA.
Edward Francis, 30, NFA.
Walter Hellund, 33, 737 Hamilton.
John Brakenbury, 21, 54 West Hastings.
Jack Tracy,
An unnamed juvenile,
Peter Seymour,
John McGregor.

INJURED
Police
Deputy Chief A. Grundy
Inspector Charles Tuley
Inspector Fred Lester
Detective R. Tisdale
Constable D. C. W. Ross
Constable W.G. Purdy

Strikers
Richard Rothery,
George H Wood,
Peter Kennedy,
Rothery was injured during the clash in the Hudson's Bay Store in the afternoon and is receiving treatment in hospital. The two other injured strikers were hurt in the evening and were arrested at General Hospital. None of the injuries to police or strikers are serious.

Mayor McGeer reading the Riot Act in front of cenotaph, April 1935.
CITY OF VANCOUVER ARCHIVES, ADD MSS 54 VOL 9 NO2

provincial police. McGeer began shouting, "Okay boys, you asked for it and here it is." He read the Riot Act, and after a few seconds of stunned silence the crowd began singing "The Red Flag" and marched off.

> *Then raise the scarlet standard high;*
> *Beneath its folds we'll live and die,*
> *Though cowards flinch and traitors sneer,*
> *We'll keep the red flag flying here.*

The mayor and council were convinced that what they had witnessed was an attempt by communists to get the unemployed to overthrow the democratically elected government. At ten that evening, simultaneous raids were carried out on the many participating organizations' strike headquarters, where posters, banners, pamphlets, and documents were seized. As word of the police action was circulated, crowds of strikers

Effigy of Mayor McGeer reading the Riot Act.
CITY OF VANCOUVER ARCHIVES, ADD MSS 54 Vol 9 No2, Location (503-D-1)

began to gather at the corner of Carrall and Hastings and later down the street at City Hall. Store windows were broken and hand-to-hand fighting began. The city police mounted squad, along with mounted provincial police, charged into the crowd, swinging their quirts. By midnight the crowd had been dispersed.

A General Strike was proposed for May 1, but never fully materialized. McGeer responded by making a radio broadcast blaming the communists, although in communication with the federal government, he laid the blame squarely on the feds for the failure of the relief camp system.

Although the story of the men is well known, little is known about the contribution of women, but contribute they did. The Women's New Era League had called a conference for late April to discuss the relief camp strike, comprising twenty-four delegates representing seventy-two organizations such as the Local Council of Women, the Civilian Pensioned

Mothers, The Women's Section of the Provincial Worker's Council, The Socialist Party, and several church organizations. Chaired by Fanny Cowper of the New Era League and Peggy Harrison of the Women's Labour League, a resolution was introduced by the Unemployment Relief Committee of the Local Council of Women urging the Federal government to provide a works program and immediate temporary relief to the strikers. As the conference had coincided with the reading of the Riot Act, an action committee of twelve was elected to send a delegation to see the mayor and to consider further action.

When they met with McGeer on April 25, he was only too glad to wire the deputy Prime Minister on the spot, referring to the women as among the city's best citizens and was only too happy to support their demands to the Federal Government. Meanwhile, planning for the strike had begun. On April 28, the Commonwealth Co-operative Federation (CCF) was to hold a parade and rally at the Denman arena in support of the strikers. Out of these two events, and the strong support and sympathy of various women's groups, the action committee mobilized a variety of women's groups under the banner of the Mother's Day Committee to support the relief camp strikers.

Not much is known of the thirty-seven women who attended the first meeting of the Mother's

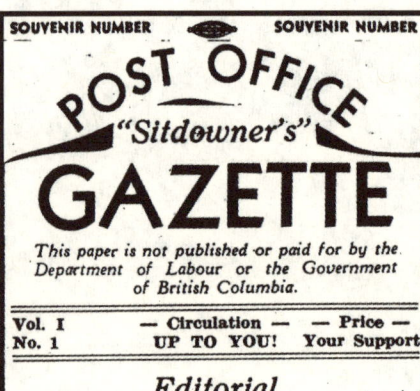

Day Committee on May 3, 1935, except that the leadership was generally left-leaning, coming largely from the CCF's Women's Central Group and the Communist Party of Canada's Women's Labour League. At the planning meeting for the Denman Arena Rally, held at the Moose Hall, the organizing ability and radical intention of the women was evident.

> *"It's up to the people to abolish relief camps," was the cry that went up from more than three hundred women assembled under the auspices of the CCF Women's Group in the Moose Hall on Thursday evening.*
>
> *"We've had enough of commissions, delegations and petitions," they shouted. "Now we'll take over and act."*
>
> ~
>
> *"Abolish the camps: don't let the boys go back," the women urged.*
>
> *Not once were the strikers referred to as such or as men; always "our boys."*
>
> ~
>
> *Shouts of "Let's go" greeted Ernest Cumber, Secretary of the Relief Camp Workers' Union, when he said he would like to have the pleasure of leading the women down Granville Street to the City Hall.*
>
> —*The Vancouver Sun,* April 26, 1935

ON THE SATURDAY preceding the parade and rally, a large contingent of women handed out twenty-five thousand tags labelled "Our boys, Are they Criminals?" in return for donations to support the strikers. Since the parade was illegal, because no permit had been given, this was also a politically astute reminder that men were being jailed for tin-canning. They also circulated a petition demanding the camps be closed.

The women also proposed that their group, led by Mother Sarah Colley, march at the front of the parade, ahead of the strikers: a clever manoeuvre to demonstrate the widespread support the strikers had and a direct message to the police that they would have to go through the women to get at the strikers. The rally of sixteen thousand people was the largest to ever attend an indoor meeting in Vancouver up to that time.

The other main group in the leadership of what would become a permanent organization was the Women's Labour League, composed mainly of communist women with branches in Vancouver, on Vancouver Island, and in the Interior. They were so radical, the Trades and Labour Congress had refused their National Federation membership, because of their strong support of the Communist International's Third Period of active participation in the labour movement. During the Depression the League was imaginative and inventive in their tactics, picketing during evictions and returning evicted goods through the back door as the sheriff was carrying more out the front. They advocated on behalf of those who were refused relief and operated summer camps for needy working-class children, eventually establishing Camp Jubilee on Indian Arm.

The committed leaders, like Lil Stoneman and organizer Annie Stewart, could hardly be labelled agents of Moscow. Although the radical imperative of the Communist Party of Canada took precedence, local conditions could not be discounted. Thus the planning of the Mother's Day Committee for a Mother's Day appropriate to the concerns of the time began to take shape, using a traditional form in a political way. As the organizing committee stated, "Such action will be something of real value instead of the bourgeois maudlin sentimentalism associated with Mother's Day." First they applied for permission to hold a tag day on May 11. They were refused, but went ahead and raised almost a thousand dollars for, as they always called them, "our boys." On Mother's Day they led fifteen hundred relief camp workers from the Cambie Grounds to Stanley Park. Three hundred women marching in time to the CCF Band, led by four women pushing baby carriages in front of a sign reading, "We the Mothers of Today Demand Abolition of the Relief Camps," entered Malkin Bowl and formed a huge outline of a heart, which was then filled by the relief camp workers. This and other examples of "militant mothering," in Joan Sangster's memorable phrase, represented one facet of the activities of what would soon turn into The Mother's Council.

The committee followed up their Mother's Day Action by sending a delegation to see Mayor McGeer, who refused to see them. They then buttonholed him in the hallway and, when prodded, he responded that he would not follow the law of God, as they proposed, and feed the men. So they went to Rev. A. Roddan, a champion of the unemployed, who had scheduled the mayor as a speaker to his congregation, and demanded he cancel the mayor's appearance. When he refused, they attended the service en masse and when McGeer rose to speak they all walked out. The next week they marched to City Hall and demanded another audience with the mayor, who was not in. So they occupied the police station until Chief Foster assured them that all "their boys" would be fed and have a place to sleep.

Their next actions occurred during the "On to Ottawa Trek," when they successfully defended the right of strike leader Arthur Evans' family to relief, even though he had been arrested as a member of an illegal organization, the Relief Camp Workers' Union. Slowly the non-left and even the CCF withdrew as the immediate crisis waned.

One result of these conditions was an increase in undercover police operations, which later (June 18) gave the police warning of a longshoreman's protest on Ballantyne Pier. With members of the RCMP and provincial police on hand, Chief Foster prepared and equipped his troops well for the ensuing tear gas attack, which was followed by a charge of the Mounted squad. Striking longshoremen were gassed and clubbed while attempting to establish picket lines and persuade scabs to join their strike. The legal right to picket was suppressed simply by decree of Police Chief Colonel W.W. Foster. Next, the Citizen's League commandeered the Armouries and formed an auxiliary police force of 160 armed, blue-shirted men who were turned loose on the waterfront to help the Shipping Federation maintain "law and order." Even with all these resources at their command, they were still unable to break the strike until early December.

The militant actions of The Mothers' Council never completely stopped and their talents and energy would be called for again. In 1938, as the province stopped paying its share of make-work project money and shut down its work camps earlier than usual on May 1, and logging camps closed early due to hot weather, another major confrontation began to build. The breaking point came when Mayor Miller dropped single men from the relief rolls, claiming the city could no longer afford the massive bills. Council also passed a bylaw banning "tin-canning" and 108 men were arrested and sentenced to serve time at Oakalla. On May 11, sixteen hundred demonstrators occupied the post office, a federal facility; the art gallery, a provincial institution; and the Hotel Georgia, a privately owned business.

The men at the Georgia Hotel took five hundred dollars cash for food and left almost immediately. The other occupations dragged on for over a month, until June 20. This strategy depended on outside support for food, which was provided by the Mothers' Council, who had once more decided that conditions demanded a contingent coalition with the Commonwealth Co-operative Federation (CCF) women. They formed the Women's Emergency Committee to Aid the Single Unemployed. Betty Kerr was chair, and secretary was Effie Jones, the perpetual Communist Party candidate for mayor. The women organized and made it clear to the mayor that the sit-down strikers had plenty of support, interrupting a speech he was delivering to set him straight. The Operation Sit-Down Strikers, as the post office and art gallery occupiers were collectively known, recognized the importance of the women when they presented the head of the Mothers' Council, Mrs. Lusk, with a bouquet of flowers at a "sports day" rally held in the lobby of the post office.

On the morning of June 20, the art gallery was emptied by the Vancouver Police, using tear gas. The RCMP tried gas at the post office, but the men smashed the large plate glass windows from the inside and the gas dissipated. The Mounties had to go in and were met with bricks and iron bars. Demonstrators were beaten by police and the Mounted squad caused havoc. The mob marched down Hastings, smashing windows. Later that afternoon, a protest rally was held at the Powell Street Grounds and the protesters marched on the Cordova Street police station to demand the release of the arrested men. Windows were smashed but no attempt to enter was made.

Meanwhile, the Women's Emergency Committee was busy tending to the injured men on the lawn of the Ukrainian Labour Hall. At midnight, one hundred men sailed for Victoria and the women were among the five thousand at the dock pledging their support. The next night, the Emergency Committee sent ten women to Victoria to see the Premier to demand work and wages. Four of the ten were from the Mothers' Council and were accompanied by Maurice Rush, Secretary of the Young Communist Party. They were met at the dock in Victoria, then led a march through downtown while singing "Hold the Fort." After the women had addressed a meeting of three hundred in Central Park, all but two went home. Premier Patullo saw the two remaining members, along with others, but was unmoved, although eventually he did make some concessions.

The Emergency Committee also actively condemned the police brutality, writing a letter to City Council and attending the meeting where the letter was read and debated, but only because Councillor Helena Gutteridge, a member of the 1935 committee, insisted.

These tactics of confrontation, where women rallied, demonstrated and marched, as well as performed the mass work of feeding, clothing and nursing, were both militant and radical and should be remembered not as a mere sidebars to riot and mayhem, but as important and necessary ideological battles in the ongoing class war.

> **Eviction Chronolgy**
>
> **SUNDAY.**
> 5:10 a.m. --- police give warning to sitdowners to leave Post office and Art Gallery.
> 5:40 a.m. --- Eviction starts.
> 6:10 a.m. --- After half-hour battle, last man cleared out of Post office.
> 6:15 a.m. --- Smashing of windows begins and continues for at least fifteen minutes.
> 6 to 7 a.m. --- "Mop up" police squads clear downtown streets, and raid jobless head quarters.
> 1 p.m. ---C.C.F. executives and M.L.A.'s meet and demand Legislature resign.
> 2 p.m.--- Ten thousand listen to protest speakers at Powell street grounds.
> 4 p.m.--- Two thousand gather outside main police station, breaking windows and demanding release of men.
> 5 p.m.--- leaders disperse Police station crowd.
> 7:30 p.m.--- Pastors of city churches discuss eviction and jobless situation.
> Midnight---One hundred jobless leave for Victoria.

British Columbia Penitentiary under construction, 1878.
BRITISH COLUMBIA ARCHIVES A-03358

CHAPTER 4

B.C. Pen Riots 1934-1976

"Laws are political in nature...those in power make the laws that contribute to social and economic inequalities."
—RAMSAY CLARK U.S. Attorney-General
quoted in the *Matsqui News*, April 4, 1979

IN HIS OFFICIAL dispatches, Warden W. H. Cooper liked to use the French word *émeute*, meaning uprising or riot, to describe disturbances in the British Columbia Penitentiary. Following forced retirement from his position as head of the Vancouver relief department for untoward behaviour in 1928, Cooper had returned to the job as warden in 1932. On his watch, riots were soon to become a common subject of discussion both in New Westminster and Ottawa.

In general, prisons are instruments in the class war. The poor are disproportionally represented, as are Aboriginals. This means that the prison population is poorly educated, underemployed, in poor mental and physical health—in other words, marginalized. As outsiders, prisoners have literally nothing left to lose, yet they organize into effective and powerful prisoner's rights groups to negotiate with determination and fortitude for their basic human rights. It is only when they perceive that the social code in which they believe strongly has completely broken down, i.e., legitimate demands with respect to human rights and dignity are not respected, that violent confrontation ensues. Prisoners are humans, with all the basic rights that all humans are entitled to. They have committed crimes and have accepted their punishment, but in no way do they give up their essential humanity, which is so often denied them in this enactment of capitalism's penultimate sanction for faulty participation. It is an example of one class of people being oppressed by the agents of capital.

On September 1, 1934, seven prisoners refused the work they had been assigned in the mailbag room and were promptly marched back to their cells. Cooper put it down to a desire for more comfortable conditions, but *The New Westminster Columbian* newspaper added the claim that the convicts wanted wages for their labour in addition to improvements in the lives of men doing hard time in the B.C. Pen. Despite quick action by the warden, the protests did not stop; in fact, they grew. By the tenth of September, *The Columbian* reported seventy-eight prisoners were refusing to go to work (the warden claimed it was only seventy-three). They could be heard clearly from outside the prison, shouting over and over "wages, wages, wages." This, as well as hurling torrents of abuse at the prisoners who chose to work, went on for three days. The warden reported 182 broken windows, six smashed toilets, and many broken tables, chairs and beds. The ringleaders were paddled, though the number of times is not mentioned. Beginning on January 1, 1935, the federal government ordered that convicts who worked should be paid five cents per diem. This was the first riot in the almost sixty-year history of the B.C. Pen, but not its last. Although riots were infrequent events, on the inside, they were momentous occasions directly echoing events on the outside.

> "... *prisons are the way we deal with our poor, our minority groups and our unemployed, we tolerate them at our peril.*"
> —CLARE CULHANE, *No Longer Barred from Prison*

On April 20, 1963, three prisoners were seen trying to escape through the auditorium windows by a guard patrolling with a dog. When the convicts refused to stop, he fired three shots. The prisoners replied by throwing homemade Molotov cocktails at both the guard and the dog. The light bulbs, filled with gasoline, exploded but missed the target. One of the inmates was badly burned when his cocktail exploded in his face. The three prisoners then retreated into the auditorium, where they took a guard hostage and locked themselves in with fifteen other prisoners who had been left on the premises when the action started. One volunteered to act as doorman. The hostage-takers' first demand was to call in television

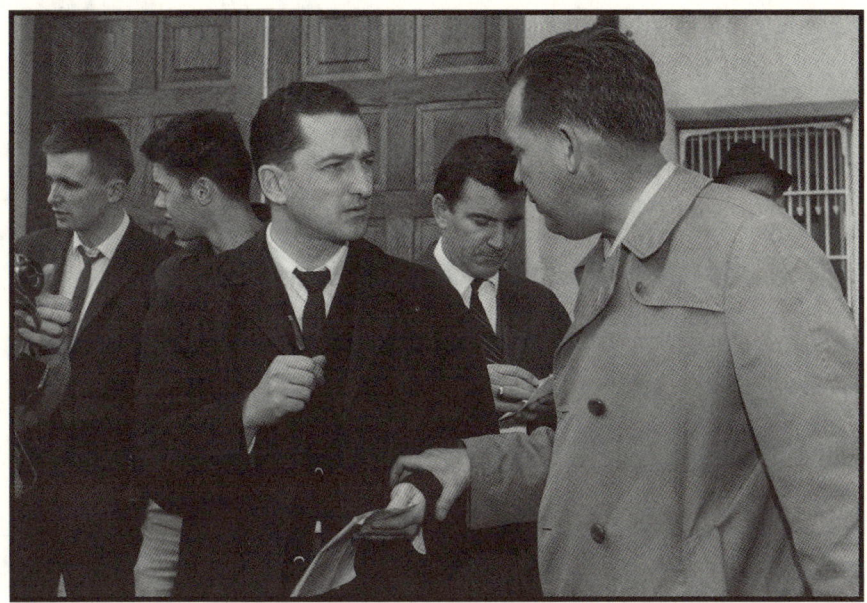

Jack Webster at B.C. Pen, April 1963.
CROTON STUDIOS PHOTO, VANCOUVER PUBLIC LIBRARY,
SPECIAL COLLECTIONS, VPL 79632

personality, talk-show host, and self-proclaimed defender of the little guy, Jack Webster, to negotiate on their behalf. For Webster's part, his best hope for any solution seemed to be that the prisoners would swallow too much "bug juice," the liquid tranquilizer supplied by the prison doctor as demanded, and nod off. Unfortunately for him, the prisoners could read and noticed the little warning on the bottle that taking too many could cause drowsiness. Some of the prisoners outside the auditorium refused to return to their cells and began wandering around breaking windows and smashing anything they could, in addition to starting fires, while the guards set about securing the rest of the prison.

The RCMP riot squad and troops from Canadian Forces Base Chilliwack were called in to restore order. Wearing gas masks and firing tear gas canisters, they managed to get all but the hostage takers back to their cells. The three were still holding the guard, meeting with Webster in the washroom of the auditorium and preparing for an attack. The prisoners, referring to Warden Hall and the guards as Nazis, seemed to fear doing time in "the hole" more than anything else and in the end their only demand was that they be transferred out of the Pen, a request which was granted for all three. Unfortunately no change was made to either the use or the condition of the hole.

In June of 1970, a twelve-member parliamentary justice committee condemned the B.C. Pen as "ancient, medieval, outmoded and ill-equipped." After the death of an inmate in August of the same year, about three hundred prisoners—dissatisfied with the official report of cause of death as cerebral haemorrhage, and adamant that a beating by guards was the cause of death—refused to return to their cells after exercise and began throwing rocks and recreation equipment—such as horseshoes and baseball bats—at the guards. Some officers were hit and the windshields of police cars parked outside were smashed. The convicts charged the ten-foot-high fence and lit fires. More than two hundred guards and police were called in, while troops stood by on full alert in Chilliwack. The prisoners were demanding an end to skin searches and they wanted to be able to appear before the justice committee to air their complaints about the Pen and its notorious "hole." At three the next morning, the riot squad went into action, tossing tear gas canisters into the yard, forcing about two hundred inmates back to their cells. The rest had backed up to the wall to avoid the gas and had to be subdued by the blasts of water from high-pressure hoses.

On the following Sunday, a Yippie-sponsored protest march from Queen's Park in New Westminster loudly demonstrated in support of the prisoners and tossed cigarettes, candies and other goodies over the fence, including a Brazilian book on guerrilla resistance tactics.

The Columbian reported on Saturday, October 6, 1973, that a ten-hour rebellion with much attendant damage had been quelled. Apparently, the incident was over the resignation of the recently formed Inmates Committee, which was supposed to be able to take inmate complaints directly to the penitentiary director, the new name for the warden. The guards were also unhappy, but blamed overcrowding, requesting that the population be reduced to four hundred and fifty from six hundred.

These two complaints were only the tip of the proverbial iceberg. Escapes and hostage-takings were on the rise, highlighting a sharp division between corrections officers (guards) and classification officers (social workers) about the way prisoners should be treated. This also mirrored the public debate as to whether prisoners retained basic human rights upon their incarceration.

The June 9, 1975 hostage-taking by three inmates and the subsequent killing of classification officer Mary Steinhauser, which occurred when marksmen stormed the vault where the prisoners were barricaded, placed the debate back on the front pages. In the negotiation phase of the hostage-taking, two unusual demands, in addition to the ever-popular request for drugs, were made. The original demand was to be flown to Algeria, the site of exile of Black Panther Eldridge Cleaver. The inmates also wanted a member of the Communist Party of Canada Marxist-Leninist wing included on the negotiation team. As the coroner's jury pointed out, the main cause of the action was the fear on the part of the inmates of spending any more time in the "hole." Or, as one of the hostage-takers put it, "going back to solitary was a 100% chance of ending up dead... taking hostages was a 95% chance of dying and a 5% chance of getting out."

> *"Canada doesn't have to execute people anymore, just sentence them to neglect."*
> —ALLAN FOTHERINGHAM, *Maclean's,* October 18, 1976

IN 1974, NINE inmates from the B.C. Pen launched a suit against the Crown on the grounds that confinement in "the hole" was cruel and unusual punishment and contrary to the Canadian Bill of Rights. The administration's name for the hole (AKA the Penthouse or the Fraserview Hilton) was the Special Correction Unit (SCU), which had been built in 1963 on the roof of Cell Block B-7 to replace the old hole in the basement of the prison. The four tiers of eleven cells each were used for three different types of "dissociation"—punitive, administrative (i.e. failure to cooperate), or very rarely, voluntary and protective, for men who could not enter the general population. In practice, other than radio, library and canteen privileges which could be enjoyed away from other inmates, all privileges were denied: no hobbies, no television, no movies, no workshops, little or no exercise, and closed visits.

> "When laws seriously encroach on human rights, they should be violated."
> —HOWARD ZINN, *Disobedience and Democracy*

The punitive dissociation cells on "F" tier, where prisoners were placed for punishment, measured six-foot-six by eleven feet two inches deep, with grey painted concrete walls broken only by a solid steel door complete with a six-inch square security window. The bed was a four-inch thick concrete riser covered with a sheet of plywood and a four-inch thick foam mattress. Prisoners were supplied with a foam pillow, two blankets and two sheets. The bedding, including the mattress, was removed during the day. Each cell had a combination sink and toilet, an air vent for heat and ventilation and a radio speaker. There was no volume or temperature control available to the inmates. A recessed light in the ceiling burned twenty-four hours per day, with a 116-watt bulb during the day and twenty-five watts at night. Prisoners were also required to sleep with their heads toward the door, thus near the toilet bowl, for security reasons. The longest consecutive time spent in the hole was 754 days. This has been compared to "being buried alive in an all-steel pressure cooker."

No reason needed to be given for punitive dissociation and many activist prisoners who were considered "trouble makers" ended up on the roof. The prisoners thought that the administration, as one of them testified, "was killing us mentally, not physically." An expert defence witness, a criminologist, said, "it is a form of murder." Another described the hole as "a tomb within a tomb."

Mr. Justice Heald of the Supreme Court of Canada agreed with the prisoners and held that the hole was indeed cruel and unusual punishment and contrary to the Bill of Rights, but refused to act on the second part of the suit and issue an order compelling the director to act on his findings. Soon after the ruling was handed down, the director of the B.C. Penitentiary announced that the "Penthouse" would be immediately modified to function within the court ruling, but dissociation in the new Super Maximum Security Unit (SMSU) would continue. And continue it did, with dire consequences.

> "The B.C. Pen 'Comes Down'"
>
> —Vancouver Sun

IN THE SUMMER of 1976, 380 of the 450 prisoners housed in the B.C. Pen joined a twenty-four-hour nationwide hunger strike with the newfound support of prisoner's rights groups acting on the outside, to protest solitary confinement. Meanwhile the ban by guards was met by the director of the Pen, who declared a twelve-day state of emergency, entitling him to order the unionized guards to work overtime. The guards, members of the Public Service Alliance of Canada (PSAC), had a list of twenty-four demands, including cutting back on inmate recreation time, open visits, and the institution of surprise searches. Through their union, the guards also put everyone on notice that they would run the institution as they saw fit and if that meant more lock-up time for inmates, then so be it.

The complete list was characterized as non-negotiable and contained conditions that could only have one outcome. That was the infamous B.C. Pen Riot, which proved to be the beginning of the end for the hundred-year-old institution, which had been promised for nearly thirty years. The prisoners would later claim that they had accomplished in twelve hours what the Federal Government couldn't do in fifty years.

Tensions between guards and prisoners were escalating. The Inmate Committee had spent the previous two months in a letter-writing campaign with over a hundred letters going to Ottawa with no response. Included was a letter to *The Vancouver Sun* signed by over two hundred B.C. Pen prisoners asking that Security (PSAC guards) be placed outside the fence with whatever weaponry they deemed necessary to prevent escapes, so long as they were moved out of the inner operations of the prison. This would thus reduce the danger they were exposed to, the overtime they were forced to work and the turmoil they used to justify their position. Sometime during the third week in September, the Inmate

Committee had passed notes to two successive shifts of guards asking for a meeting to try and talk things out. The prisoners felt the mostly older, hard-line guards had prevented any negotiations by intimidating sympathetic guards into remaining quiet. No such meeting ever took place.

> *Writing of the Criminal Justice System " ...it works systematically not to punish and confine the dangerous and criminal, but to punish and confine the poor who are dangerous and criminal."*
>
> —JEFFREY H. REIMER,
> *The Rich Get Richer and the Poor Get Prison*

SHORTLY AFTER THREE on September 27, 1976, as prisoners were being let out of their cells for showers, they overran the 240-cell East Wing and began to destroy the cell block, tearing out bars, wedging open doors and forcing the guards to evacuate the area and attempt to contain the riot to this one section. At about seven that evening, ten inmates invaded the kitchen and took two guards hostage. As the inmates smashed everything they could, the rest of the prison, including the hole, was relatively quiet. The final tally would include twenty-five of ninety-five cells in the North Wing destroyed, fifty of 110 in B-7 destroyed and two hundred in the East Block destroyed.

The newly formed Citizen's Advisory Committee was to receive its first test. A small group of appointed politicians, lawyers, criminologists, and journalists all interested in prison reform issues were joined by prison reform activist Clare Culhane. As many of the nine-member group as could be contacted were called to the prison to serve as intermediaries between the Inmates Committee—who now controlled most of the penitentiary—and the Administration. In all, six were able to attend. Meanwhile, two six-man RCMP tactical squads of sharp-shooters were moved into position. They were joined by thirty-eight riot squad officers and others were to follow.

The inmates initially demanded dexedrine for themselves and tranquilizers for the hostages. They were adamant that the Citizen's Advisory

B.C. Pen: Shortly after 3:00 PM on September 27, 1976.
PETER HULBERT PHOTO / VANCOUVER PROVINCE

Committee be present, as they desperately wanted to avoid a repeat of the Mary Steinhauser hostage-taking incident. This was to be the first time ever for a group of citizens to take an active role during an actual crisis. The next day, Clare Culhane was forced to resign from the Citizen's Advisory Committee and she agreed in order to allow negotiations to begin. Culhane was at odds with the rest of those on the committee who were present. They refused to issue a statement outlining some of the horrors they had seen on the guided tour the Inmate Committee had taken them on when they first entered the prison after the riot. The most contentious issue appeared to be the guards venting their rage by hosing down SMSU prisoners, depriving them of food, clothing, and heat. Eventually, male members of the CAC were allowed upstairs to view conditions in the hole with the IC, where they observed several inches of water on the cell floors and prisoners in their underwear or naked.

At least twice during the incident, the CAC was advised to leave the area as security was going to be restored by troops and police with clubs and tear gas. Their refusal to back down probably prevented loss of life, as certainly many prisoners had said they were ready to die.

Shortly before six the next morning, the Inmate Committee issued a statement blaming the administration and guards for failing to meet with them and resolve outstanding issues, particularly around segregation of inmates. Meanwhile, heavily armed troops from CFB Chilliwack began to take up positions around the prison perimeter. Late the next day, prisoners released one hostage as a show of good faith and in order to be allowed to meet with the media and publicize their grievances. Bad food, poor programs, and guards who resisted change and provoked confrontation to back up their contract demands headed the list. The Inmate Committee wanted to be able to meet with prisoners in the SMSU or hole at the prisoners' request or be allowed a weekly interview in order to ensure the prisoners being held in administrative dissociation were being treated properly. Mail tampering would be stopped, the inmate committee would be allowed to continue, transfers would be granted and there would be no reprisals. The media was allowed to visit what was essentially a demolition site with a hand-painted "under new management" sign in red on bed sheets that had been hung from the bars. Another banner hung on the bars read "Solidarity." According to Clare Culhane, this was never mentioned in any media report.

The Inmate Committee and the Citizen's Advisory Committee continued to negotiate with the deputy director and his team. Talks continued until 3 a.m. Thursday, when a partial breakthrough was announced; however, it was not until one the next morning when a nine-point agreement was reached, bringing an end to the riot. Early on the morning of October 2, 1976, the members of the Citizens Advisory Council left the B.C. Pen.

Three days later, an open letter was released by the Commissioner of Penitentiaries stating that it was up to the "Canadian Penitentiary Service discretion whether the so-called Agreement is to be honoured in full, or in part, or at all." Not much later the CAC was gutted, becoming little more than an extension of the John Howard Society, a prisoner advocacy group.

The East Wing was to be partially repaired at a cost of $500,000, in order to bring the population back up to 412 from the 316 it had been since the end of the riot. The next summer, there were hunger strikes protesting the lack of open visitation and the unchanged conditions in the hole, but never again would there be a riot of these proportions in the B.C. Pen, as it would cease operation in 1980.

One of the last incidents at the B.C. Pen involved a hostage-taking which ended with two of the hostages being charged as accomplices. The two women were acquitted, with the crux of the court case resting on the right or obligation of prisoners to use any means available to attempt to escape from solitary confinement, which had been declared cruel and unusual punishment and a violation of the Canadian Bill of Rights.

The last word on the riot belongs to one of the hostage takers at his sentencing hearing, at which he blamed guards demanding better pay and job security for the riot. Refusing to prepare a defence he declared, "When inmates in a prison can no longer negotiate peacefully to have their complaints and grievances heard by Ottawa and the public, then they will do it violently because they know you understand violence."

The Georgia Straight, 1971.

CHAPTER 5

Gastown Riot 1971
Rolling Stones Riot 1972

Marijuana leads to heroin, alcohol leads to the suburbs.
—GRAFFITI

SOMETHING WAS CHANGING during the Sixties. The children of the post-war baby boom were experiencing a different culture than had their parents. The Grey Cup Riots of 1963 and 1966 and Hallowe'en riots throughout the '60s seemed to herald a culture of change. By 1967, juvenile crime, an "alarming increase" in the use of marijuana, and increasing experimentation with LSD so alarmed Vancouver's police that the Youth Squad was increased to eleven uniformed men and women. Armed with public speaking skills and having attended lectures given by the Department of Psychiatry at the University of British Columbia, as well as training about the new chemicals and how to recognize the symptoms of drug usage, the squad worked closely with Vancouver School Board staff to improve relations between students and police. One of the dog squad members was trained to sniff out the illicit plant. Naturally, arrests for possession of the killer weed were soon common. These tactics revealed the two generations to be light-years apart in both attitude and anxiety.

From the summer of love mantra "wear some flowers in your hair" to Dr. Timothy Leary's advice to "Tune in, Turn on and Drop out," there was a clear message that an alternative social order was challenging the accepted establishment, complete with a new and shocking anti-establishment rhetoric. Authorities were alarmed to discover that these were their own children. Police were soon being referred to as "Pigs," a Black Panther/Yippie elision of *Animal Farm* anthropomorphism and Maoist critique. "Capitalist Pigs" was another invective thrown around with increasing frequency, although not always a great degree of accuracy.

Increasingly, the sentiments expressed in these phrases were voiced in underground newspapers such as Vancouver's *The Georgia Straight*. Founded mainly by poets and artists, *The Georgia Straight* was named so *The Vancouver Sun* would mention them in every issue when they published wind warnings for Georgia Strait, or so they said. Of course the *Sun* changed the wind warnings to the Strait of Georgia. On the surface, the *Straight's* preoccupation with rock n' roll, dope, and fucking in the streets would lead to nothing but harassment. Underneath, however, was a consistent, if uneven, critique of capital and its many excesses. Whether it was obscene or libelous, it seems the real danger stemmed from the forthright and vehement attack on the monopoly of capital everywhere, from the business of the press to the business of the church. The targets were many and easy to hit, which aroused a concerted and excessive wrath among the powers that be. Even a casual review of the *Straight's* first few years of publication shows an alarming pattern of persecution. Stepped-up enforcement of both drug and censorship laws with their attendant police brutality, redevelopment (for profit of course) and ecology were the key issues. Beginning with the persecution of the Advance Mattress Coffee House, as addressed in poet Milton Acorn's inaugural *Georgia Straight* column in May of 1967, to the Hudson's Bay Company's "No Hippies Allowed" in 1968, Stan Persky's arrest, to the Yippie and Students for a Democratic Society (SDS) occupation of the UBC faculty club. These actions were accompanied by the notorious police activities best represented by RCMP drug officer Abe Snidanko (AKA Sergeant Stedanko in Cheech and Chong's *Up in Smoke*) and the expropriations to build the Georgia Street Viaduct, not to mention Greenpeace and SPEC activities. A very clear "us and them" dichotomy began to exist. The underlying differences came down to essentially one of capitalism versus a kind of anarcho-socialism. However, these were not members of the Canadian Communist Party, Marxist/Leninist wing, or Maoists out to replace capitalism with an even more repressive communist dictatorship. In fact, it is hard to discern an actual politic, except to say it was definitely a peace- and freedom-loving anti-authoritarian uprising in the middle of a highly developed capitalist state. As Ralph J. Gleason pointed out in a prescient

December 1968 *Rolling Stone* article, the movement was "maybe so open, in a curious way, that it will be just as possible to make millions out of it by espousing revolution as it is by manufacturing mace."

Locally, Gastown was singled out as "an area of free exchange in a milieu of corporate cannibalism" in a May 1970 article in *The Georgia Straight*. By this time, when the Prime Minister of Canada, a hep cat by the name of Pierre Trudeau, enjoined young people to "see Canada first," Vancouver was the Canadian centre of hippie culture and the prime destination for many young men and women. Kitsilano, including the hostel at Jericho Beach, Gastown, and The Four Seasons Park, a squatters' encampment at the entrance to Stanley Park, were the focus of both repression and resistance.

The protest year began in May with an occupation of the Hudson's Bay Company store at Granville and Georgia for their refusal to serve hippies at their lunch counter, by the Vancouver Liberation Front (VLF). Police were called to eject the demonstrators, carting off those arrested for assault and/or trespass to the City Jail on Main Street. By that night, protesters had surrounded the station demanding their release. Police were called in to prevent a feared occupation of the building and were immediately pelted with rocks and eggs. Eventually, as the police went into the building two at a time to suit up and return in full riot gear, the riot squad was assembled. It took about three hours before the order was given to clear the streets. No further arrests were reported that night.

The next day, many of the same people led by the VLF mounted an invasion of the U.S. After penetrating some two-and-a-half miles into American Territory and returning along the railroad tracks at Blaine, the protest ended with a trainload of new cars that just happened to be entering Canada being bombarded with rocks and bottles and pounded with fists and clubs as it slowly rolled along, the new corporate reality hauled by the old industrial behemoth.

In June of 1971, the riot squad was called upon to clear the Four Seasons property, a waterfront redevelopment site at the entrance to Stanley Park that had been claimed as a people's park and camp. It was to reopen a year later when people scaled the walls and tore down the barricades and renamed it All Seasons Park. In July, there was a week of pitched battles between young people and police after the Sea Festival Riot. In October, the "Battle of Jericho" was fought on the beaches of Kitsilano between police and the occupiers of the Jericho Youth Hostel, who refused to leave when evicted. The War Measures Act was declared in October by Pierre Elliot Trudeau and seven people were arrested in Vancouver for distributing Front de Liberation du Quebec (FLQ) literature and Mayor Tom "Terrific" Campbell celebrated by launching a roundup of hippies and others that offended him. This was also the year that the drinking age was lowered from twenty-one to nineteen and marijuana and hash busts surpassed heroin arrests. It was also the year police decided to get out of their cars. By January of 1971, the first steps toward "community policing" were underway. The year was shaping up to be a busy one. As Joe Swan summarized it, "there were over seventy street demonstrations to police, men were continually being taken from their regular patrol duties. Riot equipment became almost standard uniform."

If this doesn't sound much like community policing, it's because there was another policing component called "Saturation Patrolling" that was very much at odds with the stated goals of community policing. In the Gastown area it was known as "Operation Dustpan," implying that human filth would be simply swept from the streets. A large number of police would occupy an identified trouble area, closing off the exits and detaining and searching everyone within the confines, violating civil rights and employing often brutal methods of enforcement. According to some observers, Gastown was like a police state that summer. North Shore Investigations and Security Company, a private security firm, offered local merchants a private-sector solution to rid the area of the "immediate drug problem" which included as its third and final step, to "start walking all over people." According to poet George Stanley, this "final solution" for Gastown was approved and supported by Mayor Tom Campbell and his unceasing need for publicity, fuelled by his "indifference to the needs of the community and even to the possibility of violence."

In this highly charged and tense atmosphere, various Yippie-inspired organizations such as the Gastown Dopes proposed the first annual

Grasstown Solidarity Smoke-In and Street Jamboree for Saturday night August 7, in Maple Tree Square, closing their *Georgia Straight* article with a somewhat cryptic yet ominous invitation to "sow the wind and reap the whirlwind."

Undercover police intelligence on the drug squad saw this as something more than simply a demonstration in favour of the legalization of marijuana. They prepared for an event they felt was being used as a cover by more radical groups to incite a massive confrontation with police, complete with logistics and weapons stockpiled for the inevitable attack. The organizers were billing it in *The Georgia Straight* as a high-energy spontaneous event, with nothing planned beyond music and speeches. Still, they were prepared for a heavy uniformed and plainclothes police presence, but hopeful the police would go only as far as containing the crowd.

The mainstream media offered up the high-pitched squeals of one Jack Webster (who, according to his own estimation, had been "covering hard drugs in this town since 1948"), and the detailed reports of drug use among young people on his daily radio show. In an interview with *The Georgia Straight*, he outlined his reportorial methods, the interviews with doctors, the Coroner, and a number of experts on both sides of the marijuana question, including two members of the Vancouver Police Department who were kind enough to inform this seasoned investigator that drugs were out of control in Gastown, much to his surprise. None of his informants prompted him to make any differentiation between "hard narcotics" such as heroin and "soft drugs" such as grass and hash, when in law there was no difference. Naturally enough, this led to an interview with, as Webster referred to him, His Worship Mayor Tom Terrific. Webster described Campbell's reaction as "his normal hysteria" and immediately made the connection to the actions of the Police Commission, headed by none other than the mayor. Webster claimed he was opposed to police brutality whenever and wherever he could find it, but he also knew who would be to blame if things got out of hand. The police were nervous, the mayor was hysterical, the media was in a high state of anticipation, and the hippies were in a festive mood.

On the night in question, students from Langara College arrived with a twenty-foot joint made out of straw; others had rolled a kilo of grass into a gigantic bomber. Many of the area's "hip merchants" supported the Smoke-In and wanted the business that a less oppressive atmosphere could bring. People, many wearing Rocky Raccoon masks at the suggestion of organizers, danced to the recorded music of the Grateful Dead and Jefferson Airplane, sucking on some of the three hundred supposedly LSD-laced fudgsicles handed out to the crowd. In actuality, organizers had purchased two hundred creamsicles from Palm Dairy at a discount. Organizers and others delivered speeches in support of the decriminalization of marijuana and got the crowd chanting, "Fuck Campbell, Fuck Campbell."

The police chief approached the fire chief and asked that the fire department hose down the demonstrators. The fire chief refused, stating: "We fight fires, not people." Meanwhile, just around the corner, the full riot squad was standing by, along with members of the mounted squad. At the sound of breaking glass, or so he claimed, Inspector Abercrombie ordered them to move in and clear the streets. If there was a warning, no one heard it. For many of the middle-class kids in the crowd it was their first contact with police brutality. And according to witnesses it *was* brutal; the crowd felt the full force of nightsticks, fists, and boots. Most frighteningly, horses were used to chase people into doorways and truncheons were then used indiscriminately by the mounted squad. Undercover police beat kids and hauled them to waiting paddy wagons by their long hair. It was just the excuse needed to remind the two thousand people in the crowd just who was in charge, what the rules were, and who made them. It also served notice on the rest of the community. The Vancouver Police Department was out of touch. Twelve citizens were hospitalized, seventy-nine taken into custody, thirty-eight were charged. A *Vancouver Sun* reporter claimed he was beaten. It also signified the end of an era of innocence, best characterized by the Partisan Party's (a quasi-revolutionary successor to the VLF) declaration of war on Police Chief John Fisk and the formation of the People's Patrol to combat what they referred to as the "growing power of Fascism."

Characterized as a "police riot" in the media, the police were also criticized for overreacting by the Dohm Commission, which was set up to investigate the riot. The organizers of the Smoke-In were also criticized as "dangerous and intelligent young men" partially responsible for the riot. Was that ice cream dosed with LSD? Weren't the raccoon masks to disguise identities? Wasn't the whole thing a clever plot to expose the Vancouver Police Department's stone-age attitudes towards drugs, hippies, sex, and dissent? Hadn't the Le Dain Commission recommended legalization of marijuana years ago? The police, however, steadfastly maintained that they were the ones in danger from these stoned freaks and lazy hippies and the boxes and boxes of rocks they had allegedly gathered and packed up and secretly carried all the way up through private staircases to the roofs of the privately owned buildings surrounding Maple Tree Square. Somebody must have forgotten to tell the crowd there were rocks on the roof, or maybe they just forgot to start throwing the rocks they had so carefully placed there? Or maybe there were no rocks, except in the overactive minds of the police? Certainly organizers deny the presence of any rocks anywhere. Cartoonist Rand Holmes in his *Georgia Straight* comic, "Harold Hedd," places the blame, surprisingly, not on the cops, ("Cops are all the same") but squarely on "the policy makers—like Tom [Campbell] who decide whether or not to keep them on the leash." And, of course, police communications systems were also found to be woefully inadequate and would require a large sum of taxpayer money to upgrade.

The implications seemed clear: any threat to the hegemony of the city's power elite would be met with extreme violence. Tom Campbell was re-elected in December of 1971—so much for any backlash—but retired the next year to go back to his development activities. In a curious bit of electioneering, Andrew Thompsen Campbell ran as "Tom" Campbell against Tom Campbell and received 4,922 votes. He was busted for assault and selling LSD to a policeman on election night.

Campbell's arch enemy, *The Georgia Straight*, was in the middle of a long and contentious battle between those in favour of collectivization, or co-operative ownership of the paper, and the sole proprietorship of

Dan McLeod, who argued that it was more important for the paper to continue and didn't believe that it could under collective or co-operative ownership. After the initial occupation of the *Straight* office, a second underground paper, *The Georgia Grape*, began publishing in competition with *The Georgia Straight*. *Straight* owner Dan McLeod asked for and received a court order preventing them from using the word *Georgia* in the title, becoming *The Grape*. The collective that ran *The Grape*, which became *The Western Organizer* and finally *The Western Voice*, came out of the *Women's Liberated Georgia Straight* and the *Yellow Journal* (later *The Terminal City Express*), were a determinedly anti-authoritarian bunch, but hardly hardcore Marxists or Maoists.

The dispute would eventually be resolved in favour of the "hip businessman," and local activists would turn their attention to organizing a ten-thousand-strong march of high school students on the American Embassy to protest nuclear testing on Amchitka Island in Alaska.

As a kind of coda and comment on these events, at the Rolling Stones concert at the Pacific Coliseum in June of 1972, a railway spike fired from a homemade bazooka/cannon shattered the sternum of Officer Stan Ziola and the "Rolling Stones Riot" was one for the books. This was not, however, simply a spontaneous event that got out of hand, as riots are usually characterized by the media, but a pitched battle between the Clark Park Gang and the Vancouver Police Department riot squad. Police undercover drug agents learned that the "youth" gang, mostly working-class eastside kids who were into stealing cars, dealing dope, and performing the odd B&E, was planning some sort of confrontation during the Stones concert. Rumours of up to two hundred weapons buried in the park were also making the rounds. There were also stories that the gang had counterfeited two thousand tickets to the concert and that they would be attending one way or the other. This concert also established a high-water mark for ticket prices, at five dollars per head.

A crowd of the ticketless had gathered outside the sold-out concert yelling to be let in: "Free the music." The plate-glass windows and doors were smashed and the crowd fought their way in against badly outnumbered staff members. The riot squad then formed at one end of the forecourt and were met by a barrage of rocks and bottles. As the riot squad moved forward, what was left of the crowd, presumably some of the Clark Park Gang, moved from the plaza to the darkened grassy area next to Renfrew Street and began to throw Molotov cocktails and fire their cannon. That dispersed any spectators and the mounted squad cleared out the rest. Twenty officers, including Ziola, were injured and two bomb throwers were arrested by undercover police who had infiltrated the crowd. People leaving the concert were kindly reminded by the mounted squad to watch their feet as they walked among the broken glass. That was the first the crowd was aware of the events outside.

Apparently, Vancouver residents were stunned by these events, but of course they were never told the full story in the mainstream press, who had been invited to stand by the riot squad during the melee so they could report on just what a terrible riot these no-good, but unorganized, rock and roll criminals had incited. We get good description, with plenty of bombs bursting in air, but no story, no narrative, and certainly no critique. The involvement of the Clark Park Gang is only mentioned in one publication, the history of the Vancouver Police Department, *One Hundred Years of Service*. One has to give them credit for actually mentioning most of the riots in their first one hundred years, apologizing for some, and standing firm on others.

Wave of rioting after Grey Cup disgrace to city

By ALAN HARMAN

Every type seemed to be at the police station Sunday. The rich and the poor, the sorry and the blasé.

At the inquiry desk the clerks were almost run off their feet.

"I want to bail somebody out. Where do I go?" was nearly always the question.

On the second floor a justice of the peace had an almost impossible job. He had to process applications for bail and deal with a hundred and one other questions.

There were people wanting to lay charges against other people and people who had laid charges wanting to have them dropped.

For most of the day a queue filled the public area of the court office.

VISITORS' PASSES

"My son has been arrested on an unlawful assembly charge. How do I go about getting to see him?"

Visitor's passes were filled and, in between, the telephones rang almost continually.

Ages of the arrested rioters ranged from 18 to 19.

"How shocking," said one woman when told her young son was under arrest and charged with drunkness.

"Does she mean it was shocking her son was drunk or shocking we arrested him?" a clerk asked as the woman marched away.

The revellers, who Saturday night had been so full of fire

Some Grey Cup statistics not from the Game

Here is the box score of charges laid by the police during the Grey Cup festivities, from 3 p.m. Friday to noon Sunday:

Intoxicated:	249
Unlawful assembly	28
Fighting:	15
Impaired drivers:	13
Damaging Property:	6
Obstructing police:	3
Assault:	3
Reckless driver:	1
Drunk driver:	1
Total:	319
In drunk court Saturday, celebrators were called.	139
Suspended sentence:	88
Charge dismissed:	1
Charge withdrawn:	3
Fined:	8
Jailed:	5
Remanded:	3
Forfeited bail:	31

'I'm okay,' says Willie

B.C. Lions' star halfback Willie Fleming spent a restful day at home Sunday, recuperating from a crushing tackle that forced him out of Saturday's Grey Cup game at Em-

By TOM HAZLITT

Vancouver's Grey Cup week end passed into history early Sunday with a shabby sequence of riots and disorders that reaped the city a harvest of bad publicity coast to coast.

Perfect weather, a sparkling parade and a football game in the classic tradition set the stage for a triumph of good planning and festivity.

But before the celebration was over, a hoodlum element took over and turned sections of the city into a shambles. A grand total of 319 persons were jailed, scores suffered minor injuries and scattered vandalism ran into thousands of dollars.

RIOTING ERUPTS

The game itself ended in comparative quiet, as a capacity Empire Stadium crowd watched Hamilton Tiger-Cats beat the Lions 21-10. Lions fans, so hopeful earlier in the day, retired to lick their wounds at downtown cocktail bars and private parties.

For a time, Vancouver — temporary football capital of the world — seemed quiet.

Then it erupted in a burst of juvenile mob violence.

About 200 police stood their ground against a barrage of eggs, bottles, stones, tomatoes and insults.

DOGS USED

Twice the police were forced to call out their full comple-

Vancouver Sun, November, 1963.

CHAPTER 6

Sports Riots

GREY CUP RIOTS
1963 & 1966

IN TERMS OF number of estimated participants, and certainly number of arrests, the Grey Cup Riot of 1963 is the largest riot in Vancouver history, with the 1966 Grey Cup Riot not far behind. It is also probably the least significant, in that not much really happened; even the police said it did not get "out of hand." In late November or early December of each year, the Canadian Football League holds its Championship game in one of the league cities. Football fans from across the nation gather for what is fondly referred to as "the national drunk." This event certainly lived up to that billing. In 1963, the game was held on November 30 at Empire Stadium between the hometown BC Lions, who were the Western champs, and the Hamilton Tiger-Cats from the Eastern Division. The Saturday afternoon game began with a minute of silence for the recently assassinated John Kennedy. The weekend was cold and wet and Friday night festivities brought a few arrests, as did Saturday afternoon downtown. The real action started Saturday night after the game. About ten o'clock, a woman was hit in the head by a flying beer bottle. Police, who were already patrolling the Castle Hotel beer parlour, went after the bottle-tosser and were roundly booed when they tried to haul the offender out of the bar. Once out on the street, it went from bad to worse. Bottles and rocks were thrown at the police, who called in reinforcements. Granville and Georgia was a battlefront. Three hundred and nineteen people were arrested between three on Friday afternoon and noon Sunday, 249 being charged with being drunk in a public place and twenty-eight with unlawful assembly. Most were between the ages of eighteen and twenty-four; the legal drinking age was twenty-one. Other arrests were for fighting, obstruction, assault, damaging property, and a few driving offences. There were also thousands of dollars of property damage; apparently sections of the city were a shambles. The more than two hundred police were bombarded with eggs, rocks, bottles, tomatoes, and insults. At least twice the police called out their dogs. Barking and snarling on command, wearing spiked riot collars and held on six-foot leashes, the dogs lunged at the crowd until they began to move. Soon, however, it was last call in the jammed beer parlours and the streets were filled with drunks. It took until well after midnight before police, on foot and motorcycles, along with the dog squad, were able to restore order and get traffic moving again.

The newspapers seemed to take the view that this was just part of the celebration, publishing the names and addresses of those arrested and covering the scene at the police station where the rioters were being bailed out, as if it were a party. The police, of course, promised to be better prepared next time, but insisted that the situation was never out of control and they never had to think about resorting to "other methods of holding the crowd."

The Grey Cup was held again in Vancouver in 1966, when the two Roughrider teams, Ottawa and Saskatchewan, played on Saturday, November 26. This time over three hundred were arrested before the game even started. The Grey Cup parade was held Friday night, winding twenty blocks through downtown from the starting point at the north end of the Burrard Bridge. Most of the action happened along Georgia Street between Hornby and Seymour, about an hour after the end of the parade. At one point during one of the three major battles, police ordered what the newspapers referred to as a "green alert" for all units to converge at once. The three pitched battles comprised 150 city police and RCMP marching shoulder to shoulder, being showered with bottles while attempting to clear the pavement of crowds of up to four thousand people. While some people were throwing bottles from hotel windows, others were uprooting street signs, tearing down flags and decorations, tearing ornamental garbage cans from their supports, and smashing windows. By the end of the riot the battleground was ankle deep in broken glass and about thirty-seven were treated in hospital emergency wards. None were seriously injured. One fifteen-year-old girl arrived home in Southeast Vancouver wearing handcuffs and the police had to be called to release her. There is a complete list of those arrested, this time mostly for unlawful assembly with the remainder for drunkenness and malicious damage. The coverage is not as playful and the blame is placed squarely on "hoodlums" who all look to have regular addresses in the city and the suburbs. Two solutions offered were to discontinue bidding for future Grey Cups and beefing up the riot squad.

No mention is made of the prohibition-era liquor laws and the repressive social milieu, but it might be useful to pay attention to the next major sports riot in Vancouver for some further illumination.

STANLEY CUP RIOT
1994

"...compared to major riots elsewhere in the world, many experts would see the Robson Street incident as less like a riot and more like a large, unruly house party."
—Riots, A Background Paper:
The City of Vancouver Review of Major Events, September 1994

ON THE NIGHT of June 14, 1994, forty to seventy thousand people gathered on Robsonstrasse, in the retail heart of downtown Vancouver, to celebrate the seventh and deciding game of the Stanley Cup finals being played between the Vancouver Canucks and the New York Rangers. Vancouver lost the game and a riot erupted. Rocks were thrown at police, windows were smashed, and stores were looted. The next day, newspapers were filled with reports of amateur insurance adjusters estimating the millions of dollars of property damage incurred and the usual "few bad apples" song and dance that characterized the riot as an "L.A. type event" and had destroyed the city's reputation as a world class city.

City of Vancouver pamphlet, 1994.

Before the glass was even swept from the streets, Vancouver City Council called for a community-based review, which would focus on preventing a recurrence of similar incidents. "The purpose of the City's review is to look at the issues underlying riots and how they can be influenced." The scope of the review would be strictly limited, however, ostensibly to make the research "manageable." Race riots, religious riots, and riots related to political issues were not included. "For the same reason, the team did not research the social causes of disaffection and violence."

> *"We are not going to give the city up to ransom to a few trouble-makers."*
> —MAYOR PHILIP OWEN

By September of the same year, the research team had whipped together *Riots, A Background Paper: The City of Vancouver Review of Major Events*. The research team consisted of the Directors of the City's Risk and Emergency Management Division, The City of Vancouver's Finance Department, The Division Head of Newspapers and Periodicals for the Vancouver Public Library, another VPL Librarian, a constable from the Community Services Section of the Crime Prevention Unit, and the Vancouver Police Department. They authored an internally inconsistent document full of information, carefully footnoted and attributed. Because of the research team's self-imposed limitations, the document is incomplete and fails to impart any useful knowledge on the cause of riots.

The background paper characterizes the Stanley Cup Riot as a house party that got out of hand. Alcohol and the media were blamed. The media invited the revellers and then gave them a venue to put on a show. Alcohol was the accelerant. Despite being well prepared, the police didn't handle the whole thing very well and the various branches responsible for public safety were unable to communicate with each other. A Richmond resident quoted in the paper states, "It didn't take a psychic to predict what would happen." Does this mean that, given the circumstances, there would certainly be a riot, or that the police would not be ready for large-scale crowd control?

> "The Stanley Cup riots brought these limitations into stark perspective. While staff had planned for a potential disturbance—the Emergency Operations Centre had been activated and personnel from the RCMP were on stand-by—when the event occurred communications were a limiting factor in the response. Fire units provided through mutual aid from other municipalities were equipped with incompatible communications systems. Vancouver Fire and Police units teamed with Ambulance units to respond, but had to maintain physical contact since radio communication was impossible across agencies. RCMP units were unable to communicate on scene with Vancouver Police. It is a credit to our emergency response personnel that the incident was managed so successfully under these circumstances."

[FROM AN ADMINISTRATIVE REPORT TO VANCOUVER CITY COUNCIL, JULY 2, 1997 FROM THE PROJECT COORDINATOR AND PROJECT MANAGER EOCC/AREA WIDE RADIO PROJECT, ON BEHALF OF THE CHIEF CONSTABLE AND GENERAL MANAGERS OF FIRE AND RESCUE SERVICES, ENGINEERING SERVICES, AND PARKS AND RECREATION SERVICES.]

The background paper does not address the possible social causes of violence and disaffection, which ironically is often the "background." This curiously bland document tries to make the case that riots can occur anytime, anywhere, when large crowds of people get together to celebrate with either too much police presence, or not enough. Either way, a riot is defined as the isolated act of a small band of party animals who get their kicks smashing, burning, and looting and the Stanley Cup Riot "was so volatile and so uncharacteristic of Vancouver that it raised a concern that what happened on Robson Street could recur in conjunction with any large event." Witness the summer of '99 and the unlawful search and seizure of liquor at SkyTrain stations during the Symphony of Fire, or New Year's Eve 2000, when police spokesperson Anne Drennan warned citizens to stay away from downtown (the police chief later apologized for this high-handed approach). This begs the question: how can an out-of-control house party cause so much fear and near-panic in policing circles? Maybe the analysis is wrong. Maybe the cops know something they're not telling us. Maybe they do understand the underlying causes but don't want us to know what they know. Whether we call it conspiracy or ideology, if one is really interested in understanding the causes of the riot, one might actually have to look at the event in context and not as some weird anomaly that couldn't and shouldn't happen here.

PART I

BARBARIANS AT THE GATES

EVEN A CASUAL look at the location, participants, and actions of the rioters tells quite a different story. A cursory examination of police action in their function as protectors of private property, versus ensurers of public safety, is the first clue. The crowd gathered at the corner of Robson and Bute, the site of some of the most expensive retail space in Canada. On the southeast corner behind scaffolding and plywood hoarding, a Banana Republic (later a Footlocker) was under construction. This was a time when the business community was pushing the slogan and idea that Vancouver could and *should* become a "world class city." When the Whitecaps won the North American Soccer League title in 1979 over New York, television commentators referred to Vancouver as "a village by the sea." Conveniently, Robson Street is well served by public transit, including the SkyTrain, which enters a tunnel when it gets downtown and accesses a network of underground malls serving to deposit suburban shoppers throughout the retail core. SkyTrain functions as a retail shopper delivery system designed to transport willing consumers and queue jumpers alike into the heart of capital. Jump the SkyTrain to Granville Station and emerge into the bargain basement of Canadian capital, the Hudson's Bay department store. Take the tunnel over to Eaton's, ex-home of the nation's bankrupt shopkeeper, now a Sears. Customers and/or shoplifters spill out onto Robson across the street from the Vancouver Art Gallery and the courthouse, past what was then Duthie Books (now-defunct) flagship store and the old library, then along the richest retail block in Canada. No longer the Robsonstrasse of quaint European shopkeepers and restaurants but now the outposts of multinational designer-label stores where few workers can afford to shop: Calvin Klein, Roots, and the new Banana Republic. The motto of the Downtown Business Association seems to be, "if you can't afford to shop, then don't come downtown." Did those crazed suburban bastards misunderstand the invitation? When the media invited the citizens of Vancouver to "celebrate your Vancouver Canucks," those who were implicitly excluded did not understand that they were not really citizens and therefore were not at all welcome at any civic function. Alongside the ostentatious consumption you have street people—poverty in the midst of plenty. However, the invitation was both informal, i.e., word of mouth, and open; no RSVP required.

People came downtown for several nights running during the playoffs with few problems. But when the bars emptied after the final game was lost, the crowd on Robson Street was much larger than expected, shutting down traffic. The police made the decision to disperse the unruly crowd, using dogs and tear gas in order to escort a fallen comrade to an ambulance. Construction rubble from the Banana Republic site was the main weapon of choice. According to police spokesperson

Anne Drennan, "We did not move in in any way with the crowd control unit until we felt we were losing control, until we felt it was absolutely necessary." In other words, "losing control" and "absolutely necessary" were the same thing. The police chief later claimed there was no time to read the Riot Act, which is historically the mayor's job anyway. The mayor was out of town in New York, at a hockey game, losing his bet with their mayor. One wag speculated, "That's where all the salmon went, Phil Owen lost them to Rudy Giuliani."

We're number two! Who the fuck are you?

As the police moved the crowd with tear gas and rubber bullets in a seemingly random fashion, up one street and back down again, plate-glass display windows were smashed and stores were looted. Cars, including police vehicles, were flipped onto their roofs. Masked men in balaclavas with cell phones roved the streets, easily avoiding police who were busy trying not to be caught alone and were always vastly outnumbered by the crowd. The whole thing was over in a matter of minutes, rather than hours, and everybody went back where they came from. Arrests were made later, for the most part using videotapes taken by police or seized from media outlets. The whole thing was televised live, with local media feeds going international from the surrounding rooftops up and down Robson Street.

I went to a riot and a hockey game broke out.

Half of those arrested were unemployed, and ten percent had no fixed address. Three-quarters came from outside of the City of Vancouver. Most were young, single white males with previous criminal records. Super shoppers all. Not exactly a marketer's dream of the ideal consumer.

Hockey is all that is left of public discourse.

So while the young, extremely well-paid Canuck left-winger almost deconstructed the New York defence, hardly anyone outside of the art and poetry crowd was deconstructing the Vancouver of the mid-nineties. If they had, what they would have seen was the culmination of a frightening drift into a corporatist city state of wealthy entrepreneurial capitalists, talking on cell phones while driving Porsches and honking at squeegee kids to get the hell out of the way.

> *"First you have to beat them in the alley."*
> —CONN SMYTHE

Funny, I went to a riot the other night and a hockey game broke out, but really, I couldn't tell the difference. Men in protective equipment swinging sticks, fanatics in the crowd yelling encouragement. Rules being broken pretty much with impunity. What would be aggravated assault anywhere else is two minutes in the jug, with time off if the other team scores. Why aren't the cops seizing film and pressing charges after every ugly stick-swinging incident? Sanctioned violence between hired gladiators implies permission in any crowd. If Pavel Bure can get away with it, why can't I? Capital knows no rules. It's no accident that the top TV and radio stations, in terms of advertising revenue, were owned by the same people who owned the hockey team. That's entertainment, but it ain't the symphony, as the hockey club advertised. No, sport is merely a part of the culture, rooted in violence with its attendant values of racism, homophobia, and sexism embedded within the power structure. Real fans catch the spirit: the spirit of violence and transgression. If the city's theory was correct, there would be a riot after every game because all the conditions necessary were present. That's not the case, however, but why?

> *"The Rocket Richard Riots are an example of spontaneous agency."*
> —JEFF DERKSEN

Hockey is a game of transgression; the end justifies the means. Any real hockey fan could intuit these basic unspoken rules, and would want to be part of the "game." So, in fact, the real fans were down on Robson Street, fighting for the home team in the trenches, plundering the opponents' warehouses for ammunition. So who's confused? Just a few simple-minded small-time capitalists whose yearly take equals the sales of concessions in one overtime intermission, which is why we have GM Place and grossly overpriced tickets, while the real fans are out on the streets, shut out, homeless, and about to be penalized.

PART II
WHAT REALLY HAPPENED? ANOTHER VERSION.

THE MAY 25 issue of *Terminal City*, a local "underground" or alternative free distribution newspaper, ran a cover with the headline "Hockey Night in Vancouver" in bright red flaming letters superimposed on a burning city, with a flaming Canuck logo followed by the words, "show your team spirit." The production values are not great; I was told something went wrong with the colour separations, but if the message is not clear, a page-four column—with the author's name curiously dropped out, more production problems I'm told—titled "Canuckmania?—Booze up and Riot!" and subtitled "OR BRIAN WILL LOOT YOU" will make clear the prescience of at least one local rag. A meditation on the joys of hockey and beer drinking with a none-too-gentle nod to the homophobic violent nature of the great Canadian game, the column also contains an invitation to "start your window shopping now. There are two liquor stores and a handful of bars to pillage, so courage should not be a problem."

> "But in the meantime I'll be happy to see the Canucks win the Cup because Brian needs a new CD player. I'm talking Booze Up and Riot. I'm talking LOOT, LOOT, LOOT! I'm talking Robson Street the night the Canucks win. I'm talking Christmas for poor adults."

The column ends, "Yes, hockey is a great game, but it is after all, only a fucking game." Some five hundred posters of a similar nature were plastered around the city core. Incitement to riot or poetic licence? The police thought the first. Crown Council, who would actually be the ones to lay any charges, refused to proceed. Of course the City's researchers did not have access to the *Terminal City* material because the VPL did not archive this particular magazine and why not? Perhaps their masthead slogan might provide the best indication: "The Subject Who Is Truly Arbitrary To The Chief Magistrate Will Neither Advise Nor Submit To Loyal Means." This is just the kind of attitude Mayor Owen, who practised governance by photo opportunity, deplored in his vision of Vancouver as a "world class city" with the emphasis squarely on "class."

Since the days of displacement for Expo 86 and the leaky condo crisis, the city of Vancouver has stepped up the war on the poor, with periodic crackdowns on squeegee kids, panhandlers, and buskers. Changes to the Unemployment Insurance and welfare system have left the social safety net in tatters. Community policing is still just a buzzword, there are more food banks than McDonald's in Canada, and the poor just keep getting poorer and more marginalized. A recent study by the Vancouver Planning Department predicts that the City of Vancouver can "safely" accommodate up to twenty thousand homeless people with little or no diminution in quality of life. Now *that's* world class. In most cities they're called "ghettoes" and are objects of civic shame, but seldom is there an effort made to redistribute the wealth accruing to a world class city. The poor are left with little or no choice about anything.

Whether there were four hundred rioters, as police and media claim, or four thousand, as one participant told me, seems immaterial. A bunch of street kids were tired of being harassed by a surly and demoralized Vancouver City Police Force.

In the aftermath of the riot, in a column titled "Riot, Shmiot, I deny it," Brian "Godzilla" Salmi takes the time to tally the score: "The cops didn't have anything to do with it. It wasn't the mayor's fault. The merchants didn't serve the booze. The rioters didn't start it." He also cleverly lays blame for the "Booze up and Riot" column on "enemy" journalist Brian

Kieran, who he claims faxed the column with his name on it in order to get Salmi in trouble. He also characterizes the looting as a "hyperactive consumer frenzy just a little weirder and wilder than Bay Days or Midnight Madness at Value Village."

In his column, Salmi gives the first word to his comrade and erstwhile accomplice Hammer the Neo-Barbarian, in a twisted take on civic pride that shoots holes in Vancouver's world class city concept: "Any city can riot when they win, but we're the first motherfuckers to riot when we lose."

One year later, the Canucks and Salmi were at it again, with a clear invitation to destroy Yaletown, in an instant replay of the Stanley Cup Riot. The class politics are even more inescapable in this passage:

> *This year it's time for all those smug, arrogant, pretentious, Capers eating, BMW driving, Holt Renfrew wearing, studio dwelling, cocaine snorting (learn to cook that shit you fools), Anne Rice reading, Chanel smelling, Rolex timing, Seinfeld watching, condo flipping, latte sucking, Gucci bagging, Details subscribing, business partner swindling, pre-nuptial agreement signing, RSP buying, Whistler skiing, credit card maxing, Evian swilling, chartered accounting, tax evading, Liberal voting, Yuppie swine who live in Yaletown to feel the wrath of Vancouver's disaffected youth. So here's a word of advice to all you Capers eating, BMW driving...etc., etc.: do yourselves a favour (I'm sure you're familiar with that concept) and book yourselves a little vacation time toward the end of June. Sail off to your Gulf Island retreat, drive up to your Whistler hideaway, jet off to Club Med, take that eco-adventure safari in the Himalayas you've been planning, or go visit your parents in Arizona, but by all means get the hell out of town, 'cause your little dream world is going to smell like tear gas for a couple days (and don't think that's going to be an easy scent to get out of your leather couches).*

If that ain't class war, I don't know what is. This invitation to ongoing violent action against the owners of private property, as opposed to business owners, illustrates where the conflict with the systematically disenfranchised—the have-nots—occurs and reads like a call to arms for an ongoing revolutionary movement, based on class. This is where the riot meets the revolution. However, the question remains: Can the propertied members of the working class ever form common cause with the less privileged?

Staff Sgt. Hugh Stewart briefly turns away from TV monitor at APEC inquiry showing him pepper-spraying protestors at Gate 6 during APEC protests at UBC in 1997.
IAN SMITH PHOTO / VANCOUVER SUN [PNG MERLIN ARCHIVE]

CHAPTER 7

APEC RIOT 1997
RIOT AT THE HYATT 1998

THE ASIA PACIFIC Economic Cooperation forum, or four nouns in search of an adjective, as some would have it, was held in Vancouver at the end of November 1997. For six days, between eight and ten thousand journalists, corporate CEOs and government officials were to make the APEC forum the biggest event that Vancouver had hosted since Expo 86. Government officials and those in the tourism industry saw it as a rare opportunity for international media exposure, a chance to promote Vancouver's many charms all around the Pacific Rim. Vancouver beat out Calgary to host the event in a good old-fashioned bidding war reminiscent of recent Olympic bids, hoping not only to boost tourism and strengthen the city's profile in the Pacific Rim, but to garner the $23 million of direct and spin-off income that experts in this kind of forecasting estimated would be spent in the city between November 24 and 30.

APEC had its beginnings in 1989 as the Association of South-East-Asian Nations, formed by the leaders of six Asian nations as a private "club" to discuss issues of mutual interest in an "Asian way." In 1989, an Australian initiative to open up the club to others with interests in the area was the final push that founded APEC. The leaders of many Asian countries were particularly sensitive about being members of any body that might actually criticize the way their countries were run, or more specifically, the way they ran their countries. Despite the high-powered economies involved, its mandate remained very low key, at least until the Seattle round in 1993 when, for the first time, the leaders of all the member economies actually attended and the rush to globalization was begun in earnest. By the following year, APEC had emerged as a powerful force in the fight to establish a free-trade zone in the Pacific Rim. Part of the reason can be seen in the way the meetings were organized and presented to the various leaders. Summits are an order of international meeting that only recognized countries can attend, so the APEC meetings were billed as a forum, not a summit; the distinction between countries and economies would allow Taiwan and Hong Kong, both of which China would want to represent at any summit, to attend. The leaders could then negotiate liberalized trade without losing face by signing any binding agreements, or entering into treaties with sworn enemies.

Although the organization makes no formal agreements and passes no resolutions requiring compliance (including trade-dispute resolution mechanisms), consensus agreements are negotiated that do much to liberalize trade. Aside from any issues with global capitalism, the mere presence of dictators like Indonesian President Suharto and China's Jiang Zemin would guarantee protests from human rights activists almost anywhere in the world. Add in concerns for workers' rights and the environment and you have a virtual guarantee of massive, broad-based, well-organized demonstrations.

APEC would break all Canadian records for numbers and costs of security. The recent history of APEC is one of protest and high security throughout the world. Manila as host city in 1997 put twenty-six thousand armed guards in place; Osaka used even more in 1995. The City of Vancouver budgeted $1.5 million for police security, while overall costs for police protection were estimated to run about fifteen million, according to the RCMP. Overall costs for the six-day free-trade extravaganza would run to over sixty-four million dollars. The Vancouver-hosted APEC forum would require over three thousand police officers, both RCMP and City of Vancouver, as well as two thousand private security guards, not including the secret services of the countries represented, who would provide the protection their leaders required.

Protection from what? Opposing free trade in general as being bad for workers and protesting the human rights records of some of the participating "economies" would be a variety of non-governmental organizations representing various degrees of radicalism and militancy.

The People's Summit, the most mainstream group and in receipt of $200,000 from the Government of Canada, was supported by the

Canadian Labour Congress and the United Church, as well as others. Fronted by ex-federal NDP leader Ed Broadbent, The People's Summit was to mount public meetings, educational forums, arts events, and rallies. Delegates who represented opposition viewpoints were being brought in from many of the participating countries to add their voices and report on the local effects of free trade in the developing economies at home.

The NO! to APEC Coalition was planning to turn out in full force as they had a year earlier when they demonstrated to protest the APEC meetings in Manila with a nonviolent march on the Philippine Consulate in downtown Vancouver.

On the more radical end of the spectrum, APEC-ALERT, an approximately twenty-member coalition, was planning full-scale civil disobedience, not only to protest against the aims and methods of APEC, but also to protest the presence of APEC on the grounds of the University of British Columbia. The president of UBC had invited the leaders to the campus without consulting students and staff, some of whom felt that by allowing the university to be used as a meeting place lent not only credibility to APEC, but also gave the whole free trade movement an undeserved boost. It might be worthwhile to remember that Jiang Zemin of China had turned down an honourary degree from the University of Victoria several months before the APEC forum, after a storm of protest against China's human rights record and particularly the continuing repression in Tibet. Now Jiang Zemin was heading for Vancouver to be honoured at a $200,000 gala civic dinner where he would give the keynote address.

> *"We will be getting arrested."*
> —APEC-ALERT co-organizer JAGGI SINGH

Security officials feared a repeat of the protests against APEC at the forum in Manila a year earlier, when ten thousand people stormed police barricades and battled police in the streets with sticks and stones, pipe grenades and Molotov cocktails. In Vancouver, in a departure from usual practice, the decision was taken to set up special demonstration zones guarded by riot squads near the important forum sites. Of course, these would be the very best locations where protests could reasonably be expected to take place. According to the RCMP, "we'll allow some access, but definitely not direct access...the public has rights, but we're not going to jeopardize the leaders." In other words, people could protest, but could do nothing the people whose very presence was being protested would ever see. Some organizations, including the British Columbia Civil Liberties Association, were concerned about what they saw as flagrant violations of their civil rights in the planning stages of the APEC forum's security. Nothing like this level of security had been seen anywhere in Canada, let alone Vancouver. If officials wanted a confrontation, they could guarantee it by denying citizens their rights of association and free speech in the name of ensuring the security of elderly dictators preaching a free trade doctrine that many opposed because of its perceived bias in favour of multinational corporations.

The arrests began as early, when two UBC students were arrested on September 23 for painting a line on the pavement at the university to outline an APEC-free zone, around the Goddess of Democracy statue that commemorates the victims of the Tiananmen Square Massacre. The REFUSE APEC campaign stated that their objective was to gradually enlarge the APEC-free zone to eventually include the Museum of Anthropology on the far western edge of the campus, where the leaders were to meet in late November. They were also planning teach-ins and other anti-APEC activities on the campus.

> SAY BOO TO APEC
>
> —slogan painted on atrium glass

Next, three students were arrested on Hallowe'en night for writing anti-APEC slogans on the windows of University President Martha Piper's brand new atrium at her on-campus home during a nighttime protest. The atrium was chosen because the University President would be greeting the APEC leaders there. The arrests happened after the protest and, more significantly, after the media coverage had ended. Campus security also threatened the students with suspension and/or academic discipline. The students responded by insisting that their right to free speech be respected, that what they did outside of class was their business and that they would renew their efforts to oppose the presence of APEC on campus and the APEC agenda in general.

As the protesters saw it, APEC stood for human rights abuses, poverty, and environmental degradation as multinational corporations sought to est-ablish themselves in the countries with the lowest wages and environmental standards. Others were focussing strictly on the human rights records and the suppression of pro-democracy supporters by Jiang Zemin, who was to be hosted by the city of Vancouver at an APEC-sponsored gala dinner for one thousand people. Mayor Owen said he was happy to host President Zemin's first speech in Canada because of the close economic and cultural ties Canada has with China. He was unwilling to raise human rights issues with Zemin because, in his view, that was the job of the federal government, not local politicians.

Tax receipts for the cost of the dinner would be issued so corporations could deduct the whole expense and individuals could write off a portion. In other words, taxpayers would be footing the bill one way or another for this "revenue-neutral"—as Mayor Owen described it—$1,000 a plate event. He was, as usual, representing his natural constituency of businessmen and developers. Their attitude to global capitalism is expressed in the following quotes:

> "I don't think it is a sensitive issue. Hong Kong business people are not unlike Canadian business people—they are here to make a buck. As long as there is not outright killing going on, they try to skirt around it."
> —TUNG CHAN, Vice-President, Toronto-Dominion Bank

> "There is no doubt that there are winners and losers in a global marketplace. Our job is not to spend time wishing that this were not the case: Our job is to do what we can to succeed."
> —MICHAEL CAMPBELL, *Vancouver Sun* columnist

On one side were those who saw trade as the be-all and end-all. In the middle were those who wanted to use trade to open up countries for later democratization. Trade first, human rights second. On the other side of the debate were those who would use trade as a *quid pro quo* lever for change. Of course there were also those on the fringes, a much smaller but very vocal group, calling for the overthrow of global capitalism, who could be counted on to make a noisy appearance.

The protest march through the streets of downtown Vancouver by forty-five hundred people was as carefully orchestrated as the People's Summit declaration and the NO! to APEC coalition's press conference before the march. Most upset were irate commuters who were inconvenienced when rush-hour traffic was brought to a standstill for thirty minutes.

Meanwhile, at the University of British Columbia, measures banning protesters from going anywhere near the APEC meeting sites were being put into place. The restrictions on access, many felt, went well beyond the security requirements and contravened citizens' right to protest. Those arrested in the days leading up to the on-campus meeting of the APEC leaders were asked to sign an undertaking that they would not return to campus during the remainder of the APEC forum. Besides being arrested for various offences, such as assault (for yelling in a security guard's ear) and violating security zones, student protesters were laying plans to make a citizens' arrest of Indonesian President Suharto. They wanted to charge Suharto with crimes against humanity, holding him responsible for the deaths of about two hundred thousand East Timorese. This would, of course, require entry and deep penetration into the fenced-off and well-guarded security zones which mysteriously kept getting larger and more restrictive as the meeting at the university approached.

Wednesday's protest at the university turned into a riot when the demonstrators at the front of a crowd of more than one thousand people began to climb a wire fence which was keeping them well away from the leader's motorcade route. As the wire began to peel off the fence frame, police moved in, using their bicycles as battering rams and pepper-spraying everyone within range, including media. At another location near the motorcade route, where students were sitting on the road, police asked them to disperse but began pepper-spraying them immediately, before they were even able to get to their feet. Forty arrests were made, including two well-armed Indonesian security men, who were immediately deported.

APEC is, in one way, a postmodern riot in the sense that public property was privatized and the only "broken glass" was the wire fence erected to allow the public to see, but not pass, through. Reaction to the riot was generally critical of police, with some sympathy for protesters and what was seen as the denial of their rights. But not in all corners, of course. By the end of the APEC forum, Prime Minister Jean Chretien was joking about putting pepper on his steak, a joke that most considered in poor taste and for which he would later offer a half-hearted apology along the lines of, "If I offended anyone, I'm sorry." His next visit to Vancouver more than a year later on December 8, 1998, would bring another riot, this time against both APEC and Chretien's involvement in security planning for the forum. The APEC inquiry into police activities at APEC was in one of its interminable interruptions, as some lawyer or other was pressured to resign for getting caught doing or saying something he shouldn't have. Eventually the inquiry's counsel would have to resign because he had attended a Liberal Party of Canada fundraising dinner at the Hyatt Hotel at which Jean Chretien gave a speech; same players, one year later. He was counsel to the RCMP Public Complaints Commission investigation into student charges that the RCMP had been responding to political pressure to help leaders like Suharto avoid even having to see protesters or their signs. The key question seems to be, did Chretien make guarantees to the Indonesians, or was it just a coincidence that the RCMP applied security measures that had never been practised in Canada? Were Canadian citizens, many of them children, denied their civil rights so an aging dictator could spend his time in Canada untroubled by bothersome protesters, protesters who would never have been allowed to speak or march in his own country? When the final APEC report was released, it was suggested that the RCMP apologize to protesters and that indeed there was political pressure from the Prime Minister's Office, but not the PM himself. The

RCMP have not apologized and the public has never been informed about any actual threats, or the role of RCMP undercover agents who had infiltrated the anti-APEC groups and who exactly took leadership positions in the APEC riot.

RIOT AT THE HYATT

ONE YEAR LATER, on December 8, 1998, approximately seven hundred people gathered outside a Liberal Party of Canada fundraising dinner held at the Hyatt Hotel in downtown Vancouver. Prime Minister Chretien, in his first return to the city since APEC, would be making the keynote address and people were still angry about his attitude towards the pepper-spraying of protesters by the RCMP. His jokes, and his apparent inability to comprehend the issues involved, outraged many of the protesters and others. Many protesters also recognized the inability of APEC to reform itself and were able to identify the role of global capitalism in some of the outrages carried out in parts of the world where APEC members held sway.

> *Make the rich pay!*
> *Socialism, The Better Alternative*
> —signs carried in front of the Hyatt Hotel

Police "intelligence" led them to believe the demonstration would be anything but peaceful. Perhaps it was the appearance of posters up and down Commercial Drive the day before, inviting people to a "riot at the Hyatt" and asking them to bring weapons. Protest organizers disavowed the posters. Perhaps it was the unwillingness of protest organizers to even talk to the police. The demonstrators feared being billed for police overtime if they took responsibility for the protest. All contributed to the charged atmosphere. The threat level was high: the police operational plan included several objectives, ranging from the protection of the Prime Minister IPP (an Internationally Protected Person) to providing an environment for lawful democratic protest, but also restoring

Vancouver police try to restrain crowd pushing against them at the Hyatt Regency.
PETER BATTISTONI PHOTO / VANCOUVER SUN [PNG MERLIN ARCHIVE]

the public peace as expeditiously as possible. The VPD was responsible for exterior security and 175 police officers were deployed. The hotel was placed behind barricades in the mid-afternoon by city police, who used bicycles as barriers. A protest zone was designated across the street from the main entrance to the hotel. The area immediately around the hotel was designated a restricted zone, off-limits to the general public. Eventually Burrard street was closed to traffic; there was a brief incident involving a pick-up truck delivering sound equipment to the demonstrators. It was quickly resolved. The line-up of different demonstrators included environmentalists and others not directly connected to APEC, but likewise eager to communicate with the Prime Minister.

The Crowd Control Unit was initially deployed at the corner of Melville and Burrard when protesters threatened to breach the restricted zone line. The CCU stood down when uniformed officers re-established control.

At about 7:30, fifteen to twenty of the demonstrators linked arms and broke through the police line at the hotel entrance and made a run up the driveway toward the lobby entrance. The fifty-man strong CCU riot squad was mobilized inside the hotel, just off the lobby. Drumming their batons against their shields, they charged out through the lobby to confront the demonstrators. More than a few hotel guests were surprised by this display of police/business co-operation. RCMP riot squad members waited up the street under the command of Staff Sergeant "Sergeant Pepper" Hughie Stewart, the man in charge at the protests at UBC and the main focus of student complaints at UBC for his use of pepper spray on protesters. The Field Commander announced, "Vancouver Police, this is now an unlawful assembly, repeat, this is an unlawful assembly, you must leave the area or be arrested." Very few of the protesters heard this announcement due to the VPD's lack of a decent public address system. This time, batons were used instead of pepper spray, because there were children in strollers in the crowd. Estimates of the number injured range from the police report of a low of four to the protesters' version of thirty. City Police Department spokesperson Anne Drennan claims the police were forced to act because they feared they were losing control. Protesters maintain the riot squad was never necessary, as nobody even made it to the door of the hotel, and the police line had been restored before the riot squad appeared. Police reports outline the timing of events: two minutes from the announcement to first contact between the CCU and the crowd, one minute fifteen seconds between the appearance of the CCU and crowd contact, thirteen seconds between movement of the CCU and crowd contact. According to the report, contact took the form of force, ranging from shield pushes to baton jabs, overhand baton strikes and overhead baton strikes. Direct contact with the crowd was estimated to have lasted between twenty-nine and forty-seven seconds. Eleven spectators and eight police officers were injured, according to police documents.

The protesters were soon dispersed and the riot squad, assuming their work was done for the night, stepped down. The night was not over, however, and the RCMP riot squad was later mobilized at the Vancouver police lockup at Main and Cordova, where about four hundred protesters had gathered demanding the release of their "comrades." Again the crowd was dispersed with few incidents, but the protesters had gained the front-page coverage they needed to advance their cause. Although much of the media focus had been on the violent aspects of the two riots, some protesters felt that the media exposure was worthwhile, even if only to illustrate the basic message that some people felt strongly enough about APEC to take to the streets. Others, however, were left to wonder whether the issues they wanted dealt with would be eclipsed by a discussion of police tactics in dealing with legitimate protest and that public discourse would be limited by the agenda of the media and its ownership, which certainly was not the same as that of the demonstrators. True to predictions, public accountability has been severely limited by legal manoeuvring, leaving several unanswered questions. The only questions asked by any of the subsequent investigations were whether the deployment of the CCU was justified and whether the level of force was justified. Matt Adie's report, completed as an observer to the investigation, raises several important but as yet unanswered questions. Lack of attempts to identify officers in relation to specific complaints, the absence of three minutes' warning to disperse before the CCU acted and, most damning, the failure of the report to "provide any evidence as to what actions of the crowd were riotous."

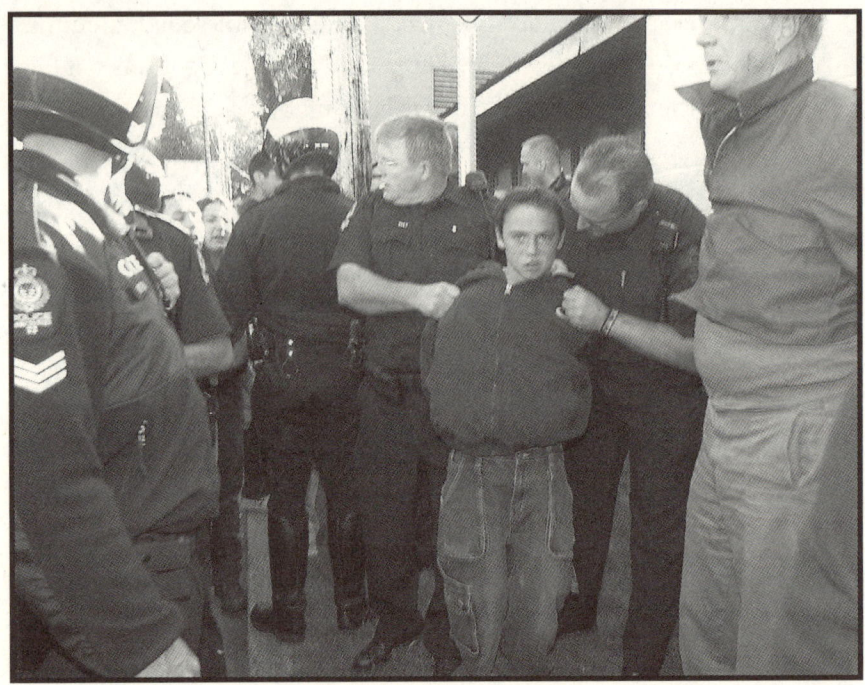

Two protesters, one a small boy, are led away by Vancouver police at the Britannia Community Centre Thursday, October 3, 2002.
JASON PAYNE PHOTO / VANCOUVER PROVINCE   [PNG MERLIN ARCHIVE]

CHAPTER 8

BRITANNIA RIOT 2002
GUNS N' ROSES RIOT 2002
PUNK ROCK RIOT 2004

BRITANNIA RIOT

SINCE COMPLETING THE first version of *Reading the Riot Act* there have been more riots in Vancouver, although there are disputes about whether any of them were, in fact, riots. Two have been referred to as "police riots," as there are those with vested interests who would prefer that the activities involved do not constitute a riot. Neither event involved the reading of the Riot Act and both involved relatively small numbers of both police and individuals. In one case, no damage occurred to private property; in the other instance, the damage was confined to one building. Both cases, however, involved long court cases. The two riots happened just over a month apart in the fall of 2002 as the British Columbia Provincial Government was in the midst of not only shifting policy but restructuring the social contract along the lines of right-wing governments worldwide. These two riots may yet become footnotes to much larger events to come.

The Britannia Police Riot, as the protesters would have it (and which may in fact eventually become the first "Gordon Campbell Riot"), occurred when protesters were removed from public property outside Britannia High School in East Vancouver, where they had gathered to protest an appearance by Premier Gordon Campbell. Although the premier was scheduled to open a Family Literacy Centre, he had already cancelled his appearance due to a protest that morning. Nonetheless, the police arrived in force. Who they were protecting and from what is unclear, and although no property damage occurred, much mayhem ensued. Not a single window was broken, but many charges were laid, including obstructing a police officer, assaulting a police officer, causing a disturbance, and unlawful assembly. No protester, and certainly no police officer was seriously injured.

According to Judge Smyth, this is a protest in three acts. The arrest of the clown, the impasse at the paddy wagon, and the arrest of an underage male. The Family Literacy Centre was scheduled to be opened by Campbell at three o'clock, on October 3, 2002. The opening was by invitation only and a small crowd of about 150 to two hundred people concerned about the educational policies of his government had gathered outside. According to the Judge's "outline of the facts," in this crowd were about a half-dozen demonstrators with "covered faces," possibly a contingent of local anarchists, some of whom appeared regularly at anti-Campbell protests. Campbell had already been given a rough ride earlier in the day at UBC, at another "private" announcement of his government's educational policies, and had cancelled his appearance at the Literacy Centre. Nonetheless, members of the VPD motorcycle and bicycle contingents showed up in force.

Just before three o'clock, the police arrested George Feenstra for assaulting one of the police officers guarding the door to the new Family Literacy Centre. The Reverend Feenstra was performing a mime and wearing a clown nose when he approached the police line. He may have accidentally brushed an officer. The clown was arrested and hauled around the corner to a waiting police wagon. A crowd had gathered demanding his release. As he was being carried to the wagon, in the words of the judge, "the handling of Mr. Feenstra was forceful, more forceful, in my view, than was either wise or necessary." Somehow his face came into contact with a brick wall. Police quickly formed a wedge to clear a path through the crowd so the clown could be placed in the wagon. Two of the people with "covered faces" moved a dumpster in front of the police wagon, others threw down pallets, and still others—about twenty—sat down in front of the police wagon. After about a half-hour of trying to get people to move, the senior police officer ordered them removed. Some were simply picked up and moved, others were subjected to "compliance techniques, methods designed to inflict discomfort or pain and secure the co-operation of the person affected." The wagon moved away followed by protesters.

Soon the melee included children, who joined the protest when nearby schools were dismissed and one young man, age fifteen, ended up being roughly arrested. Members of the crowd attempted to affect his release, to the point of pushing and grabbing the officer who was holding the boy in a bear hug, resulting in further arrests.

It is the judge's comments on the issue of unlawful assembly that are particularly instructive.

> [49] Onlookers to an arrest enjoy constitutional protection in expressing their disapproval of it, but the protection does not extend to conduct that threatens a tumultuous disturbance of the peace. I conclude that an unlawful assembly took place at Britannia Community Centre on 3 October 2002, although not everyone present took part in it. In the terms of s. 63(1): there were persons assembled there who had a common purpose in the carrying out of which they so conducted themselves as to cause persons nearby to fear, on reasonable grounds, that they would disturb the peace tumultuously. The common purpose, while it would have been differently described by most of those pursuing it, amounted to this: to interfere with the police in the performance of their duties. The evidence suggests, indeed, that some of those present may have been actuated by a kind of free-floating contempt for the police which the events at Britannia Community Centre crystallized. In any case, many of the assembly did not confine themselves to simple, noisy protest. Some threw objects at police officers, including a can apparently containing a soft drink, a bottle of water, a water-filled balloon, and pebbles or stones. Some spat at police officers. Some pushed, jostled, and kicked at them. In some cases members of the crowd jumped onto the backs of police officers. Cst. Harty was tackled and injured while making a lawful arrest. Some persons in the crowd screamed, either at

large or to the faces of police officers, imprecations such as "Die, pigs," "Kill the pigs," and "Fuck the pigs" which, in the context of all that was going on around them, contributed to the reasonable fear that this was an occasion when opposition to the police in the performance of their lawful duties, which had already expressed itself in some acts of violence, might attract more.

Judge D.I. Smyth in Part 43 of his judgement states:

> What differentiates a riot from an unlawful assembly is that a riot entails an actual, tumultuous disturbance of the peace, whereas an unlawful assembly requires only the reasonable fear that such a disturbance will erupt. At the same time, freedom of assembly is a fundamental freedom, a value whose constitutional protection is not lost only because those taking part in an assembly have become loud and angry.

In other words, the defendants who were charged with participating in an unlawful assembly were found guilty because it was reasonable to fear the possibility of a tumultuous disturbance. The question of whether there was a riot or not still remains.

Although no one was charged with rioting, people are left with little choice but to ratchet up the action as police attempt to reinstate control, lost largely due to their own actions. The judge of course has no comment whatsoever to make on Campbell's policies, so people are left frustrated.

GUNS N' ROSES RIOT

THE GUNS N' ROSES riot is another case where there is a dispute about whether there was in fact a riot. $350,000 worth of glass was broken at General Motors Place and two bystanders were seriously injured after the last-minute cancellation of a rock concert by a band from Los Angeles with no overt, discernible political agenda.

Rioters smash windows at Gate 3 outside GM Place. Fans of the music group Guns N' Roses were angry when they found out the concert was cancelled.
ARLEN REDEKOP PHOTO / PROVINCE [PNG MERLIN ARCHIVE]

Problems started when the doors to the stadium were still locked ten minutes after the concert was supposed to have started, then were compounded when the announcement was made that the concert was cancelled. Many of the speakers at the different gates were out of order so security guards were forced to shout above the crowd. There were about 7,500 tickets sold for the November 7, 2002 event. In addition to Orca Bay (owners of the hockey palace) security guards, there were only nine police on duty.

"Led by the loudest louts at Gates 3, 7 and 8, the crowd began shouting and gesturing obscenely at the police, at Orca Bay security force personnel and at television crews. After the destruction of property began, within minutes every window and door at gates 3, 7 and 8 had been broken. The vandals used steel crowd control barriers, concrete ashtray stands and metal newspaper vending boxes as battering rams, and loud cheers followed the smashing of each pane of glass."

[ADJUDICATORS' REPORT, PUBLIC HEARING ORDERED BY THE POLICE COMPLAINT COMMISSIONER]

Newspaper accounts and the adjudicators' report from the public hearing into complaints against two VPD members provide the written text, but there was a more interesting primary source, which was the Vancouver Police Riot investigation web page: <www.city.vancouver.bc.ca/police/guns&roses>. Here you could watch videotape of the events and if you cared to, help identify rioters. However, according to one of the officers in charge, the rioters are committing acts of unlawful assembly and mischief. Presumably that is because no one read the Riot Act. The Honourable Ross Collver, in his role as adjudicator in the public hearing order by the Police Complaint Commissioner under the Police Act, has no hesitation in labelling the event a riot in the very first sentence of his report, describing the police action as "suppressing a riot." He also helpfully points out the Criminal Code protections for police officers in riots.

32. (1) Every peace officer is justified in using or in ordering the use of as much force as the peace officer believes, in good faith and on reasonable grounds,
   (a) is necessary to suppress a riot; and
   (b) is not excessive, having regard to the danger to be apprehended from the continuance of the riot.

So can you have a riot without having the Riot Act read? As in most of the riots cited herein, it would seem so. The legal definition will seldom be met in the future, but the popular usage will continue.

PUNK ROCK RIOT
I WENT TO A PARTY AND A RIOT BROKE OUT
VERSION ONE
POLICE FILE #04-250903—RIOT

SEPTEMBER 25: A house-wrecking party went from bad to worse when the Vancouver Police Crowd Control Unit had to be called in. Police first attended the party at 216 E. 12th Ave. for a noise complaint and they were assured the live band inside and all the partygoers would all be shut down by eleven.

Police were called back to the house an hour later by neighbours who said the house was being destroyed and the party had spilled into the street. Officers attended and called quickly for back-up due to the number of people involved and the hostile mood of the crowd. People were chopping at the house with axes. Bottles, wood, and stones were being thrown at police. Partygoers set fire to debris they had piled in the street. The Emergency Response Team was called and all riot squad members on duty were requested.

The fire reached the height of the power lines and a transformer was in danger of being consumed by the fire. An elderly woman was evacuated from her home next door and all bystanders were removed from the area. After the Riot Act was read and two minutes passed, officers sent tear gas into the house and cleared the partygoers out. Fourteen people were arrested and charged with mischief and/or unlawful assembly. Another five people arrested were released without charges.

In all, the police response included:
25 District Three officers
33 officers from other districts
6 officers from CounterAttack
5 Emergency Response Team members
2 Police Dog members
11 Crowd Control Unit officers
3 Detective/Investigators
9 Additional
17 off-duty officers

The Richmond RCMP sent five of their members to help in other areas of the city. The Vancouver Fire Department had twenty-eight firefighters and seven trucks at the scene. Also on scene were ambulance attendants and BC Hydro staff. There was only one injury reported—a city worker was treated for exposure to gas.

The party was possibly advertised on the internet as a house-wrecking party, drawing people from all over the city and neighbouring areas. Police are also investigating a fire that occurred September 26th at one of the other houses slated for demolition on adjacent Watson Street.

VERSION TWO

PINHEAD, TERROR GNOME, AND CORPUS VILE were leading their black metal band Descention through a set in the basement of one of the houses in the punk rock compound at Twelfth and Watson. The three houses, built between 1904 and 1907, had been purchased by Holborn Developments and were slated for demolition, along with a couple of neighbouring houses, for the purpose of building a seven-unit townhouse on the site. "Kill Cops" graffiti and "Beware of Pit Bull" stickers adorned the houses, according to newspaper reports. The residents had been given an eviction notice and planned a housewrecking party for Saturday, September 25. They had been told the houses would be demolished, so they thought they would help things along. They warned the elderly woman next door and sent out invitations throughout the Northwest. About two to three hundred people characterized as "punk rockers and self-proclaimed anarchists" showed up and the party spilled out onto Watson Street, which is actually more of an alley, where a bonfire was getting underway. Police showed up at about eleven and asked the partygoers to keep it inside. They were met with bottles, rocks, and debris. Police called out the riot squad and the crowd started tearing down the house while waiting for the police to return. One witness reported seeing a man drag a fridge out of the house with a pick-axe, others ripped siding off the walls to feed the bonfire, while still others carried flaming brands into the house, lighting fires from room to room. The band played on.

Within fifteen minutes, the police had mobilized the riot squad and cordoned off four blocks around the houses. By 11:35, the flames from the bonfire were licking at the hydro wires and a transformer. At 11:46, the elderly neighbour was taken from her home and, shortly after, tear gas canisters were fired into the crowd and the riot squad came

Night after big party, a neighbour relates the evening's events which culminated in the party house being gutted.
IAN SMITH PHOTO / VANCOUVER SUN [PNG MERLIN ARCHIVE]

marching down Watson Street, banging on their shields. Forty people were arrested and held overnight while eight were charged with offences ranging from public mischief to unlawful assembly. The band got out with their equipment.

In interviews after the fact, the elderly woman next door said, "I guess they were told they could smash it all." The organizer said he planned the party intending to wreck the houses since they were now owned by a "faceless corporation and they were going to be torn down anyway." He added, "Ten people got kicked out and I think what happened was people got fed up with the corporatization and gentrification of the neighbourhood." An employee of the developer stated that they had met with the city on Friday and were told two of the three houses had heritage value and they were debating whether they could incorporate them into the plan. The next night at two in the morning, firefighters were called back to the scene and all three houses were burning. Apparently there had been a posting on the internet that promised to return and finish the job.

Monday morning, the city ordered the developers to demolish the houses. The party organizer felt the police response was an overreaction. "We were just having some fun."

It may not be electoral politics, but it sure looks like the local political economy got a workout that weekend. Rumours of heavy crack cocaine and crystal meth use by partygoers, mixed with alcohol, may have played a part in crowd actions, but the plan seems to have been inspired by one branch of anarchist philosophy. "Propaganda by the deed"—wherein a single act, such as an assassination, bombing, or riot is of such clarity that the people understand their oppression and the "weakness of the oppressor" and rise up and begin the revolution.

CONCLUSION

THE FUTURE OF RIOTING

As long as the powerful and greedy are willing to protect their ill-gotten gains with paid enforcers; as long as oppression continues to be the order of business; and as long as there are marginalized people, there will continue to be riots. Whenever people are pushed beyond the limits of endurance, they will rise up and strike back at the instruments of their oppression, taking out their rage on the private property that is at once their desire, as well as their nemesis. There is, in effect, no choice: the rich and powerful must either decide on their own to share both wealth and power—which seems unlikely—or the poor and oppressed will be forced to organize in order to seize what is rightfully theirs. This also appears highly unlikely. A much more probable scenario would have the social order remaining pretty much the same, with predictable results.

Within a representative democracy operating on basically a one-party system (capitalism) with slight shifts between the left and right wings accounting for little more than an easing of the burden on the poor and disenfranchised, there can be no other conclusion. The interests of corporate capitalism and state capitalism are not the interests of the vast majority. The middle class is created and then paid off to meet the need for a managerial class which also performs a regulatory function. The capitalist system requires a large, well-trained, and compliant middle class, as well as a large pool of cheap labour willing and eager to trade their unskilled labour for a shot at the brass ring of upward mobility. It works that way because that's the way it works. A few on top, a large stratified middle, and a constant but somewhat changeable underclass that is used as a "negative example"—both exploited and vilified, stereotyped and valorized.

It is a system run by consent on the part of all participants: everyone has a clearly defined role, and the expectation is that everyone should play their role without serious complaint. The rich must pay their "share," the middle class must do their duty, and the poor must accept their lot—which often includes prison as a regulatory device and an example. Witness the oft-repeated but never proven saying: "We are all only a paycheque away from poverty," a useful but entirely untrue instrument of economic terrorism. It is an exceedingly delicate mechanism that occasionally gets out of whack, but not often, and seldom for long. The riot is not the penultimate event heralding the revolution, but a mere corrective, a warning and a call for adjustment.

The only hope that any riot could be the precursor of social change would depend on the organization of the participants and whether they could garner any popular support for their actions. More riots more often? Not likely, but still there exists the possibility of small spontaneous actions, suggesting a larger and more ominous discontent.

CONCLUSION 135

Injured rioter outside Post Office, June, 1938.

BIBLIOGRAPHY

Abella, Irving, and Millar, David, eds. *The Canadian Worker in the Twentieth Century.* Toronto: Oxford University Press, 1978.

Anderson, Kay J. *Vancouver's Chinatown; Racial Discourse in Canada, 1875-1980.* Montreal: McGill-Queen's University Press, 1991.

Brodie, Steve. *Bloody Sunday, Vancouver 1938.* Vancouver: Young Communist League, 1974.

Culhane, Claire. *No Longer Barred from Prison: Social Injustice in Canada.* Montreal: Black Rose Books, 1991.

Kloppenburg, Anne, Niwinski, Alice, and Johnson, Eve. *Vancouver's First Century: A City Album.* Vancouver: Douglas and MacIntyre, 1991.

Knight, Rolf. *Indians at Work: An Informal History of Native Indian Labour in British Columbia, 1858-1930.* Vancouver, New Star Books, 1996.

Lazarus, Morden. *The Long Winding Road: Canadian Labour in Politics.* West Vancouver: The Boag Foundation, 1977.

Leier, Mark. *Rebel Life: The Life and Times of Robert Gosden, Revolutionary, Mystic, Labour Spy.* Vancouver: New Star Books, 1999.

Leier, Mark. *Where the Fraser River Flows: The Industrial Workers of the World in British Columbia.* Vancouver: New Star Books, 1990.

Lipton, Charles. *The Trade Union Movement of Canada, 1827-1959.* Toronto: NC Press Ltd, 1973.

MacInnis, Grace. *J.S. Woodsworth, A Man to Remember.* Toronto: MacMillan Company of Canada, 1953.

McDonald, Robert, A.J. and Barman, Jean, ed. *Vancouver Past: Essays in Social History.* Vancouver: University of British Columbia Press, 1986.

Morley, Alan. *Vancouver: From Milltown to Metropolis.* Vancouver: Mitchell Press, 1961.

Murphy, Jennifer, and Murphy, P.J., eds. *Sentences and Paroles: A Prison Reader.* Vancouver: New Star Books, 1998.

Scott, Jack David. *Four Walls in the West: The Story of the British Columbia Penitentiary.* New Westminster: Retired Federal Prison Officers' Association of British Columbia, 1984.

Scott, Jack. *Plunderbund and Proletariat, A History of the IWW in B.C.* Vancouver: New Star Books, 1975.

Stanton, John. *Never Say Die! The Life and Times of a Pioneer Labour Lawyer.* Ottawa: Steel Rail Publications, 1987.

Stohl, Michael, and Lopez, George A. *Governmental Violence and Repression: An Agenda for Research.* Westport: Greenwood Press, 1986.

Struthers, James. *No Fault of Their Own, Unemployment and The Canadian Welfare State 1914-1941.* Toronto: University of Toronto Press, 1983.

Sugimoto, Howard Hiroshi. *Japanese Immigration, The Vancouver Riots and Canadian Diplomacy.* New York: Arno Press, 1979.

Swan, Joe. *A Century of Service: The Vancouver Police 1886-1986.* Vancouver: Vancouver Police Historical Society and Centennial Museum, 1986.

Verzuh, Ron. *Underground Times: Canada's Flower-Child Revolutionaries.* Toronto: Deneau, 1989.

INDEX

A

Acorn, Milton 88

Adie, Matt 121

Advance Mattress Coffee House 88

Alexander, R.H. 29

Angler, Ontario 45

Anglo-Japanese Treaty of Commerce and Navigation 30

APEC-ALERT 113

Asiatic Exclusion League 32, 33, 34, 37, 39

Asia Pacific Economic Cooperation (APEC) 14, 23, 24, 25, 110, 111, 112, 113, 114, 115, 116, 117, 118, 119, 121

Association of South-East-Asian Nations 111

A Bill to Preserve the Peace in Vancouver 30

B

"Battle of Jericho" 90

B.C. Penitentiary (B.C. Pen) 75, 76, 77, 78, 79, 81, 84, 85

B.C. Securities Commission 43

Ballantyne Pier 71

Banana Republic 102, 103

Bellingham Massacre 32

Black Friday 60

Bowser, Attorney General Robert 31, 39

Brill, John 50

Britannia High School 123

British Columbia Civil Liberties Association 114

Browne, Major E. 33

Bure, Pavel 105

C

Cambie Grounds 33, 64, 70

Campbell, Andrew Thompsen "Tom" 93

Campbell, Mayor Tom "Terrific" 90

Campbell, Michael 25, 115

Campbell, Premier Gordon 123

Canadian Bill of Rights 79, 85

Canadian Pacific Railway 31

Canadian Penitentiary Service 85

Castle Hotel 97

Chan, Tung 115

Chretien, Prime Minister Jean 117, 118, 119

Citizen's Advisory Committee 82, 83, 84

Clark Park Gang 94, 95

Cleaver, Eldridge 79

Collver, Honourable Ross 128

Committee of 66 61

Commonwealth Co-operative
    Federation 68, 72
Communist Party of Canada's
    Women's Labour League 69
Communist Party of Canada
    Marxist-Leninist 79
Community Policing 90
Cooper, Warden W.H. 75
Corpus Vile 130
Culhane, Clare 76, 82, 83, 84, 136

D
Denman Arena 69
Department of National Defence 63
Dohm Commission 93
Douglas, Mayor C.S. 52
Drennan, Anne 102, 104, 120
Dunsmuir, Lieutenant Governor
    Robert 33, 38, 39
Duthie Books 103

E
Eaton's 103
Emergency Operations Centre 101
Emergency Response Team 129
Empire Stadium 97
Evans, Arthur 71

F
"few bad apples" 99
Feenstra, George 124
Findlay, Mayor James 54
Fisk, Police Chief John 92
Footlocker 102

Foster, Police Chief, Colonel
    W.W. 64, 71
Four Seasons Park 89
Fowler, A. E. 33
Front du Liberation du
    Quebec (FLQ) 90

G
Gambaru 45
Gastown 14, 25, 64, 87, 89, 90, 91
Gastown Dopes 90
General Motors Place 126
General Strike 67
Georgia Grape 94
Georgia Hotel 72
Gleason, Ralph J. 88
Grasstown Solidarity Smoke-In
    and Street Jamboree 91
Great Depression 62
Grey Cup 87, 96, 97, 98
Guns n' Roses 123, 126
Gutteridge, Helena 73

H
Hall, J.E. 61
Hammer the Neo-Barbarian 108
Hastings Mill 29
Heald, Mr. Justice 80
Hill, Joe 50
Holmes, Rand 93
Hudson's Bay Company (Here
    Before Christ) 64, 88, 89
Hyatt Hotel 23, 117, 118, 119

I

Immigration Act of 1907 31
Industrial Workers of the World (IWW)
  (also Wobblies) 22, 24, 25, 39, 47, 49,
  50, 51, 52, 53, 54, 55, 57, 58, 136, 137
Inmate Committee 81, 83, 84

J

Japanese Language School 35
Jericho Beach 89
John Howard Society 85

K

Kidd Committee Report 60, 61
Kieran, Brian 108
King, William Lyon Mackenzie 35
Kogawa, Joy 45
Kumeric 30

L

Leary, Dr. Timothy 87
Little Yokohama 34

M

Malkin Bowl 70
Maoist 87
Maple Tree Square 91, 93
McDougall, John (McDougall Chinee) 29
McGeer, Mayor Gerald G. 15, 61, 63, 65, 66, 67, 68, 71
McInnes, Tom 61
McLeod, Dan 94
Miki, Roy 43, 45

Mother's Day Committee 69, 70

N

Nippon Supply Company 31
Nisei Mass Evacuation Group (NMEG) 43, 45
NO! to APEC Coalition 113
North Shore Investigations and Security Company 90

O

Oakalla 72
Obasan 45
Odlum, Brigadier Victor M. 61
Okazaki, Robert Katsumasa 45
On to Ottawa Trek 71
Operation Dustpan 90
Owen, Mayor Philip 100

P

Pacific Coliseum 94
Parsons, Albert 53
Parsons, Lucy 53
Partisan Party 92
Patullo, Premier Duff 61
Pearl Harbour 41
People's Patrol 92
People's Summit 112, 113, 116
Persky, Stan 88
Petawawa, Ontario 45
Pettipiece, Parmeter 55
Pinhead 130
Piper, UBC President Martha 114
Powell Street Grounds 35, 55, 72

Propaganda by the deed 132
Public Service Alliance of
    Canada (PSAC) 81
punitive dissociation cells 80

R

RCMP 43, 66, 71, 72, 77, 82, 88, 98,
    101, 112, 114, 117, 118, 120, 121, 129
Relief Camps 12, 62, 63, 69
Relief Camp Workers' Union 63, 69, 71
Retail Merchants Association 60
Robson Street 99, 102, 103, 104, 106
Roddan, Reverend A. 71
Rolling Stones 14, 87, 94
Rush, Maurice 73

S

Salmi, Brian "Godzilla" 107, 108
Salvation Army 48, 50, 52, 53, 54
Saturation Patrolling 90
Sears 103
Shew, Lew 29
Shipping Federation 61, 71
SkyTrain 102, 103
Smyth, Judge D.I. 124, 126
Snidanko, Abe (Seargeant
    Stedanko) 88
Socialist Party of Canada 52, 55
Special Correction Unit (SCU) 79
St. John, Vincent 57
Stanley, George 90
Stanley Cup 14, 23, 99, 101, 102, 108
Stanley Park 56, 70, 89
Stewart, Staff Sergeant Hughie

"Sergeant Pepper" 70, 110, 120
Suharto, President 112, 116, 117
Super Maximum Security
    Unit (SMSU) 81
Swan, Joe 90

T

Taylor, William 53
Terminal City 106, 107
Terminal City Express 94
Terror Gnome 130
The Citizen's League 61, 71
The Georgia Straight 88, 89, 91, 93, 94
The Knights of Labour 29
The Riot Act 13, 15, 63, 66, 67,
    68, 104, 123, 128, 129
The Women's New Era League 67
Trudeau, Prime Minister
    Pierre 60, 89, 90

U

Ukrainian Labour Hall 73
Unemployment Insurance
    21, 23, 48, 58, 107
Unemployment Relief Committee 68
University of British Columbia (UBC)
    87, 88, 110, 113, 114, 116, 120, 124

V

Vancouver Art Gallery 103
Vancouver Board of Trade 60
Vancouver Club 61
Vancouver Liberation
    Front (VLF) 89, 92

W

Webster, Jack 77
Wellington Collieries 38
Western Organizer 94
Western Voice 94
Women's Emergency Committee to
   Aid the Single Unemployed 72
Women's Labour League 68, 69, 70
Women's Liberated Georgia Straight 94
Wong, Arthur 56
Workers' Unity League 63

Y

Yaletown 108
Yellow Journal 94

Z

Zemin, Jiang 112, 113, 115
Ziola, Officer Stan 94

ABOUT THE AUTHOR

Michael Barnholden

Born in Moose Jaw, Saskatchewan, Michael Barnholden is the publisher and editor of *The Rain Review of Books*. His own books include the poetry collection *On the Ropes* (Coach House), as well as *Gabriel Dumont Speaks* (Talonbooks). Barnholden is a Kootenay School of Writing collective member and he co-edited (with Andrew Klobucar) the Kootenay School of Writing anthology, *Writing Class* (New Star). A Vancouver resident since 1970, Michael works as an advocate with the B.C. Coalition of People with Disabilities.